THE BRIGHT EDGE

. . . this peculiar quality in the air of new countries vanished after they were tamed by man and made to bear harvests. . . . the air had quite lost that lightness, that dry aromatic odour. . . . one could breathe that only on the bright edges of the world . . . Something soft and wild and free, something that . . . lightened the heart, softly, softly, picked the lock, slid the bolts, and released the prisoned spirit of man into the wind, into the blue and gold, into the morning, into the morning!

WILLA CATHER
Death Comes for the Archbishop, 1927

Ponderosa pine, Zion

THE BRIGHT EDGE

A Guide to the National Parks of the Colorado Plateau

by Stephen Trimble

FLAGSTAFF: THE MUSEUM OF NORTHERN ARIZONA PRESS

Dedication

to my parents, Isabelle and Don Trimble,
who first introduced me to red rock country
and whose encouragement started me on the path
that led to this book

ACKNOWLEDGMENTS

Many thanks to the following people for their help with this book: Charles Adams, Byron Alexander, George Billingsley, Hermann Bleibtreu, Kent Bush, Steve Carothers, Kathy Foxworth, Nancy Goldberg, Dave Johnson, Peg Johnson, Karl Luckert, Ekkehart Malotki, Marc Miller, Gary Nabhan, Bob Petersen, Bob Reynolds, Don Trimble, and Mark Zarn.

Special thanks to Steve Gustafson, Sandra Mahan, Gary McClellan, Rick Stetter, and Stanley Stillion.

Design: Sandra Mahan
Editor: Rick Stetter
Production: Gary McClellan, Steve Gustafson
Lithography: Paragon Press, Inc., Salt Lake City
Typography: Tiger Typographics, Flagstaff
Color Separations: American Color, Phoenix

COVER: *The Castle, Capitol Reef*
BACK COVER: *Dawn, Balanced Rock, Arches*
All photography by Stephen Trimble, unless otherwise credited

CONTENTS

Toward the La Sal Mountains from the summit of the Waterpocket Fold, Capitol Reef

Preface: THE PLATEAU

Between here and there and me and the mountains is the canyon wilderness, the hoodoo land of spire and pillar and pinnacle where no man lives, and where the river flows, unseen, through the blue-black trenches in the rock.

Light. Space. . . . from the mortally human point of view the landscape of the Colorado is like a section of eternity—timeless. . . . I sometimes choose to think, no doubt perversely, that man is a dream, thought an illusion, and only rock is real. Rock and sun.

EDWARD ABBEY, *Desert Solitaire*, 1968

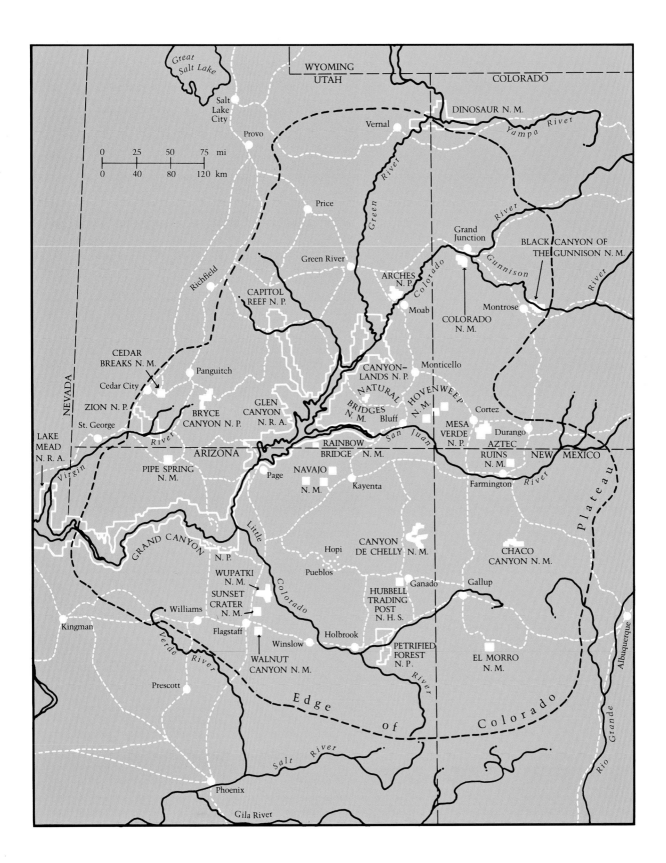

BIOLOGISTS CALL IT THE PAINTED DESERT. Geologists call it the Plateau Province. Chamber of Commerce leaflets call it Four Corners Country, Color Country, the Golden Circle of National Parks.

This is the Colorado Plateau. Red rock country. The canyon lands. A vast desert parkland of almost unbelievable beauty on the bright edge of the world.

The Plateau covers 130,000 square miles of Utah, Arizona, New Mexico, and Colorado. This great stony fragment of the Southwest harbors our greatest concentration of national parks and wilderness outside Alaska; its most famous parks—Grand Canyon, Zion, and Petrified Forest—lure visitors from all over the world.

These visitors soon discover that the entire Colorado Plateau easily could have been designated a single, gigantic park. The scenery, the wildness, the mystery stay with you no matter where you travel in the region. Indeed, the Plateau heartland narrowly missed preservation as a huge seven-thousand-square-mile Escalante National Monument in the 1930s. Today, the Plateau contains five national parks in addition to the three named above and nineteen other areas managed by the National Park Service.

The Bright Edge serves as an introduction to this national park system; since these parks preserve examples of nearly all the region's environments, it also becomes a guide to the Colorado Plateau itself. The book aims at making clear the interrelationships and continuity of park landscapes, rather than simply cataloging the attractions of each park.

These interrelationships stem from two simple facts, one geological and one biological. Any hot summer day makes apparent the great biological fact of the Plateau: *aridity.* This is a desert, where low rainfall and high evaporation rates combine to leave rocks bare, vegetation sparse, and soil unprotected from erosion.

The geological fact is summed up in the word "plateau": by definition, a huge island of relatively *flat-lying rocks,* in this case, standing between the Rocky Mountains to the north and east, and the basins and ranges of the deserts to the west and south.

This stack of horizontal layers of sedimentary rock forms the colorful "layer cake" that the Plateau rivers slice through. Each stream washes away rubble from the bases of cliffs; slowly, canyons grow deeper, with sheer, straight-sided walls. Steplike mesas and benches of land between canyons carry you across the Plateau on ascending and descending stairways of rock.

You also can call this land the Plateaus. The great geographic platform has been broken into numerous smaller platforms, including the highest of America's plateaus, which at over eleven thousand feet catch enough rain to support pine and fir forests. Here and there, island mountains rise over the red earth in snow-capped, pine-clad stillness, but no continuous mountain ranges exist here. Most of the Plateau lies at an altitude of about five thousand feet—a high, cold desert.

This rocky land isn't built for cities, for great concentrations of people. It's built for desert bighorn and collared lizards, ravens and scorpions. Once it provided a home for native peoples who could find food where explorers later would starve, who irrigated crops with trickling desert streams, who lived in houses of rock in cliff alcoves or houses of earth and brush on the plains of the open desert. Today, ranchers struggling to earn a living from Plateau rangeland must spread themselves—and their herds— across the land as sparsely as did the Indians.

Though the Plateau makes a challenging home, people easily can come here to visit, to travel, and to learn. Traveling through parks which preserve landscapes unique on the planet, they learn as much about themselves as they learn about this land they travel through, this piece of the earth which gives them life.

Grand Canyon of the Colorado River

Introduction: THE RIVERS

DAVID SUMNER

. . . the days flow through your consciousness as the river flows along its course . . . The current becomes the time on which you move. Things happen and days pass. . . . You glide on . . . unpursued, living as all good river travelers should, in the present.

ELIOT PORTER, *The Place No One Knew: Glen Canyon on the Colorado,* 1963

WATER CREATED THE PLATEAU landscape just as the *absence* of water created the Plateau lifescape. Canyons sliced from the flat rocks of the region usually are dry, but a few great rivers run year-round through the Plateau.

The master stream is the Colorado, the old, red river that gives the Plateau its name and drains 90 percent of its area. When Plateau people say "the River," they mean the Colorado, just as "the Canyon" can mean only the Grand Canyon of the Colorado. The Grand isn't the only canyon cut by the Colorado; Marble, Glen, Narrow, Cataract, and Westwater canyons all lie upriver from the Grand Canyon.

The Green River meets the Colorado at the head of Cataract Canyon, in the heart of Canyonlands National Park. Canyons on the Green include Labyrinth and Still-water in Canyonlands, Gray, Desolation, and farther upriver, in Dinosaur National Monument, Lodore, Whirlpool, and Split Mountain.

Magical names, these canyon names. Most were named by John Wesley Powell on his 1869 expedition down the Green and Colorado. When Powell and his men glided onto flat water after they shot through the final rapid in Grand Canyon, the last blank spot on the United States map had been sketched in. Their trip—the first recorded through these canyons—brought the Colorado Plateau out of the realm of myth and onto the sharply drawn maps of the geologists.

Powell's river trip first focused the country's attention on the Colorado Plateau; today much of the attention received by the Plateau remains aimed at the rivers. Each year, many thousands of people relive Powell's run through the great rapids: Hell's Half Mile, Satan's Gut, Lava Falls, and a hundred others.

Each canyon possesses unique character: the alternating friendly slickrock and stern heights on the Yampa and the Green in Dinosaur National Monument, the stark wildness and big river in Canyonlands. In Glen Canyon National Recreation Area, a segment of the San Juan River upstream from Lake Powell remains wild. And the climactic trip is the voyage starting at Lee's Ferry, Arizona, through Marble Canyon, then onward through the awesome immensity of the Grand Canyon with its dark inner gorge of ancient rock. All these canyons offer the exhilaration of great rapids, the soothing peace of gentle stretches of flat water, and intimate views of the Plateau's heart.

Float away on a red rock river and you float through time—time preserved in layer after layer of rock. Yet time as measured by a river traveler slows to match the speed of the current; the world rolls by gently in flat water as you drift under the sun. In white water, the canyon—the world—crystallizes into an instant full of nothing but churn-

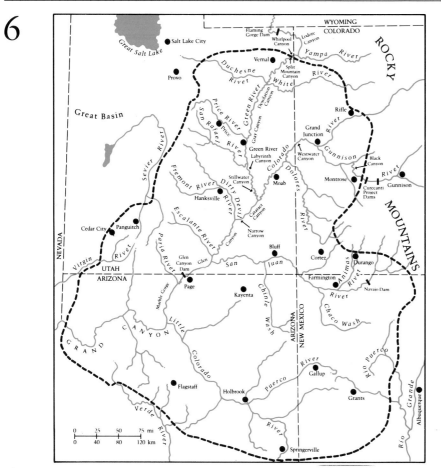

The Green River meets the red Colorado, Canyonlands

ing waves. The thrill of the rapid overwhelms every other thought. Once through the rapid, you know not whether the wild ride took a second or an hour.

Running a canyon-country river offers a unique perspective on the Plateau, a feeling totally distinct from land-bound experiences. No matter if your home lies on the prairie, in the mountains, or along the coast, when you come to the Plateau you join one of two groups: the river people and the land people. You can be both, but only alternately, never at the same time.

River people ache for moving waters, and are more at home drifting down sunlit canyons or navigating rapids than anywhere else on earth. Land people can't let a side canyon go by without demanding to stop and explore. They begrudge the places they miss as they drift by raft-bound.

Even for a die-hard land person, a river trip bestows a special feeling for the great canyons, increasing understanding of the spirit of this land. River views of the canyons resemble views from mountain valleys: you look *up* to high walls instead of peering down from rims. Indeed, these canyons have been called "the inverted mountains."

A canyon voyage changes your perspective on movement. From the rim of the Grand Canyon, its depths convey a sense of great stillness, of motionlessness. But riding the river, the canyon world *moves*. The surging river carries with it the true message of the Plateau—that the land is far from static, but rather in constant, incremental change.

The rivers and all their smallest tributaries combine to an enormous force. Here erosion acts with a power unmatched elsewhere in North America, stripping thousands of feet of rock from the Plateau and washing it downstream. Each river itself cuts only a narrow slice, barely wider than its course. In uniformly hard rock such erosion gives rise to a deep, narrow slot. In rock with alternate hard and soft layers, tributaries eat into rims and widen the canyon, the hard layers resisting erosion more than the soft, leaving great rock steps leading up from river to rim, as at the Grand Canyon.

Floating the rivers takes you through the land, not merely over its surface. Entering a canyon is akin to entering the living body of the earth, floating with its lifeblood through arteries and veins of rock, tuning your perceptions to the slow pulse of the land, single beats of river current marking the steady rhythmic changes of geologic time.

This particular form of intimacy shared with the Plateau can be had only on the rivers. It flows through your memory and leaves behind a ripple of emotion: reverence.

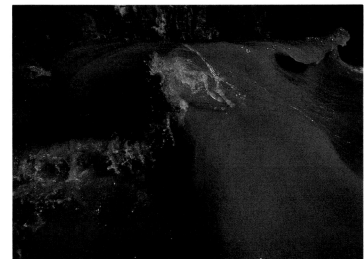

In this shifting realm of the fantastic unreal only the river is permanent. It is the one enduring mesmer from whose spectral spell no man who has once seen it is ever quite freed.

FRANK WATERS, *The Colorado*, 1946

JOHN RUNNING

Rapid, Grand Canyon

Sunflowers, Hop Valley on the Kolob Terrace, Zion

Part One: THE LAND

*Low swells of prairie-like ground
sloped up to . . . a huge monument,
looming dark purple and stretching
its solitary, mystic way, a wavering line that faded in the north. Here . . . was
the light and color and beauty. . . . a vast heave of purple uplands, with ribbed
and fan-shaped walls, castle-crowned cliffs, and gray escarpments. Over it all
crept the lengthening waning afternoon shadows.*

ZANE GREY, *Riders of the Purple Sage,* 1912

*Split Mountain is a morning canyon
. . . a pure delight of sun and water and
rock. . . . one glorious chute, rapid after
rapid, with just enough time to get your
breath in between before the line of foam
and the din downstream announce
another.*

ANN ZWINGER, Run, River, Run, 1975

DAVID SUMNER

UINTA COUNTRY
Dinosaur National Monument, Utah/Colorado

AT THE EDGES of the Colorado Plateau, the transition to surrounding landscapes occurs in spectacular fashion. On the north and east, where the Rocky Mountains border the Plateau, mountains give way to red rock country in a last great plunge of green slopes overlooking the colored flats of the desert.

Dinosaur National Monument lies astride this transition, and introduces this land of the Colorado Plateau. Here the Green River slices through the Uinta Mountains in deep canyons that pierce to the heart of the range, and then flows out into the high desert world of the Uinta Basin. At that point the Green becomes a canyon-country stream; for the rest of its length it sings of the Plateau, not of the Wyoming mountains that gave it birth.

The monument takes its name from the great reptiles whose fossils occur here in one of the earth's major concentrations. The monument's visitor center has been built against a ledge of bone-bearing sandstone, where artful quarry technicians excavate fossil skeletons just enough for the petrified bones to stand out in high relief. These animals died one at a time 140 million years ago, probably of ordinary causes, and their bodies happened to wash downstream in the local river and ran aground on a sand bar. Scavengers ate their flesh but left bones to the sun and sand, and gradually river currents buried skeleton after skeleton.

Here many bones petrified, gradually turning to stone as silica-laden river waters permeated them and replaced organic tissue with mineral crystals. Actually, dinosaurs thrived for millions of years before and after the time preserved in Dinosaur National Monument's fossil riverbank; conditions crucial for fossilization usually were missing and dinosaur bones simply decayed.

With time, the river disappeared along with the dinosaurs. New rock layers buried the Dinosaur area, the great weight of upper layers slowly transforming the river-deposited sands to the rock of the Morrison Formation. These millions of years of gradual deposition were followed by erosion that just happened to have exposed the ancient river bar when an observant geologist, Earl Douglass, came along in 1909 and discovered bones protruding from a sandstone hogback.

His discovery yielded 350 tons of dinosaur bones to museums, and the quarry site became a national monument in 1915. Some of the most famous dinosaur species lived here: the quarry has produced fossils of the powerful carnivore *Antrodemus* (better known as *Allosaurus*), plate-decorated *Stegosaurus*, and 80-ton *Brachiosaurus*, largest of land animals.

Years later, the canyons of the Green and Yampa rivers were added to the monument. You can drive to several spots on the rivers today, including Echo Park where monolithic Steamboat Rock marks the Green-Yampa confluence, and Split Mountain where the layers of rock sweep abruptly upward, sharply flexed by the rise of the uplifted Uinta Mountains. But the best way to see the canyons is to float the rivers that carved them. Though you're still in the Rocky Mountains when deep in Lodore or Whirlpool Canyon, summertime temperatures of one hundred degrees plus-hint at deserts more than mountains. Dinosaur prepares you for the Plateau country to the south.

The deepest of Dinosaur's canyons penetrate to dark red quartzite a billion years old and older, just as roots of ancient rock also lie exposed in the inner Grand Canyon of the Colorado, far downstream from Dinosaur. Great bald domes of slickrock turn up, harbingers of Canyon Country. In lower Yampa Canyon the twisting river has incised old meanders (left over from times when it flowed in a broad valley of soft earth). Today these sweeping bends carved into the hard Weber Sandstone form tiger-striped cliffs reminiscent of Glen Canyon on the Arizona-Utah border.

Piñon-juniper forests clothe the southern foothills of the Uintas, dry slopes touched with canyonland plants like buckwheat and saltbush and Mormon tea. The undammed Yampa provides rare muddy-water habitat crucial for native fish like humpback chub and Colorado River squawfish, both endangered species.

Dinosaur: a canyon wilderness with one foot on the Plateau, one still in the mountains. A special place, and also a preview of the canyons downstream, an introduction to slickrock gorges and thunderous rapids, desert bighorn sheep and whiptail lizards, Entrada Sandstone and Mancos Shale.

Formal boundaries aside, the Plateau begins at Dinosaur.

Juniper, Yampa Canyon

DAVID SUMNER

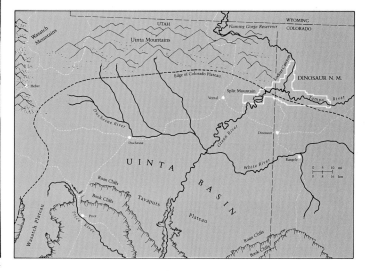

HENRY SCHOCH

Monument Canyon, Colorado National Monument

It is a lovely and terrible wilderness . . . harshly and beautifully colored, broken and worn until its bones are exposed, its great sky without a smudge or taint from Technocracy, and in hidden corners and pockets under its cliffs the sudden poetry of springs.

WALLACE STEGNER, *The Sound of Mountain Water*, 1969

CANYON COUNTRY

Black Canyon of the Gunnison National Monument, Colorado
Colorado National Monument, Colorado
Arches National Park, Utah
Canyonlands National Park, Utah
Natural Bridges National Monument, Utah
Glen Canyon National Recreation Area, Utah/Arizona
Rainbow Bridge National Monument, Utah
Capitol Reef National Park, Utah

THOUGH CANYONS CHARACTERIZE the whole Plateau, nowhere do they dominate the landscape like they do in the Plateau heartland, the truest Canyon Country. Here, every plain, mesa, and plateau ends abruptly; red rock canyons dissect them in incomparable erosional fantasy.

Boundaries for the Canyon Country are unmissable. On the west and east, high elevation forests hem in the canyons: the western High Plateaus and on the east, the San Juan Mountains of Colorado. Northward, the long, scalloped Book Cliffs, running from Grand Junction, Colorado, to Price, Utah, line the horizon; southward, Canyon Country ends not far past the San Juan River, where you pass into the arid, more shallowly eroded Painted Desert and the desert grassland of the Navajo Country.

Rivers carved the Canyon Country, perennial rivers fed by distant mountains. The Colorado forms the main trunk to which a branching network of streams attach— more branches than in any other part of the Plateau. The Gunnison, Dolores, Green, Dirty Devil, Escalante, and San Juan join the Colorado on its downstream sweep through Canyon Country. Lesser streams join each of these, and washes and arroyos lead into each lesser stream. Throughout this section of the Plateau, canyons bar travel; most pioneers and early explorers avoided it altogether. More than any other place, the Canyon Country feels like the Plateau's heart.

In the Sierra Club book, *Slickrock*, Edward Abbey pinpointed Glen Canyon as the heart of the heart, and his choice makes sense. By the time the Colorado reaches lower Glen Canyon, most major Plateau tributaries have joined it. Only the junctions with the Little Colorado and the Virgin remain downstream. Here the river has gathered its waters, marshaled its forces from the far corners of its drainage system to create with bold, absolute mastery the consummate slickrock canyon.

South Window from Turret Arch, Arches   *Fins, Devil's Garden, Arches*

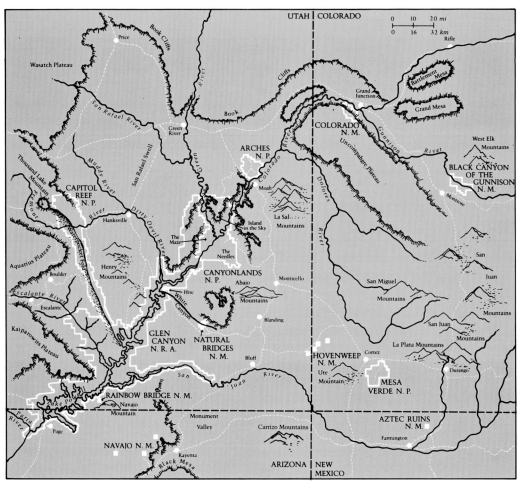

In Glen Canyon, canyon landforms reached their highest expression: slots, tapestried walls, amphitheaters, arches, alcoves, natural bridges—all the best of the Plateau lay hidden here, with the gentle river flowing through their midst. I must use *past* tense, for Glen Canyon is dead, buried under Lake Powell. And that's part of our story. But first, go back upstream and follow the canyons from their beginnings, from where they enter the Plateau. Start with the introduction, not the climax.

At the Plateau's edge in Colorado, north of Montrose, a few million years ago lava poured out directly in the path of the Gunnison River. The river had to swing south to get around this rising barrier of volcanic rock that today we call the West Elk Mountains. In its new course, the Gunnison eroded away soft sedimentary rocks and reached hard, dark, ancient Precambrian rock. Trapped, entrenched in a canyon, the river continued slicing into this hard rock, gradually carving today's twenty-seven-hundred-foot-deep Black Canyon.

With a heavy load of abrasives and an abundance of water from the nearby mountains, the Gunnison has deepened its steeply dropping course in Black Canyon in a rather short time. Small tributaries make little headway in the hard rock, so the river carves only a single, narrow main channel. In Black Canyon of the Gunnison National Monument, you get a close-up look at the huge walls of this somber canyon.

Near where the Gunnison and Colorado rivers meet at Grand Junction, more characteristic Canyon Country red rock crops out along the north rim of the great uplift known as the Uncompahgre Plateau. Here, floodwaters running down the tilted layers at the edge of the Uncompahgre have eroded a series of beautiful, steep-walled, box-shaped canyons. Today, they make a precipitous foreground for views across the broad Grand Valley of the Colorado to the shaley horizon at the Book Cliffs.

Colorado National Monument preserves this array of canyons, with isolated natural rock monuments rising from canyon floors. A paved road climbs at each end of the national monument through a stack of sedimentary rocks and up to the Uncompahgre highland. The drive between these two climbs winds along canyon rims, with the constant spectacle of canyons dropping away below.

The Colorado River swings on, past the Uncompahgre and into Utah. Near Moab, on the north bank of the River just across from the La Sal Mountains, lies Arches National Park. Here a phenomenal concentration of natural stone arches spreads across a domed slickrock upland. How many arches? The total depends on your definition of "arch," but fifty-five or so openings known as arches or windows occur here. These arches owe their existence to an unusual geologic setting.

Millions of years ago, layers of salt buried deep beneath this region tended to liquefy and flow when compressed by the great weight of overlaying rocks. Lighter in density than the rocks above, the salt forced its way upward in areas where cover was thinnest and slowly domed up rocks closer to the surface. Later erosion removed many of the upper rock layers, and groundwater reached the salt.

Percolation of water through the salt dissolved enough material to cause collapse of some domes, forming valleys on the surface (like Salt Valley in the park). Such uplift and collapse cracked rocks along the edges of the dome in evenly spaced lines (joints) parallel to the length of each dome. The forces of erosion have worked on these cracks, gradually widening them to leave fins, high slabs of the harder rock, standing in rows. Impressive concentrations of fins occur in the Fiery Furnace and Devil's Garden. Holes eroded in these fins enlarge to form the arches of Arches.

Some sixty river miles downstream from Moab, the Green River joins the Colorado deep in Canyonlands National Park. In this huge park every imaginable Plateau landscape meets in a jumble of mesa, cliff, and wild canyon. Isolated between the Green

Winter, Black Canyon of the Gunnison

Wherever we look there is but a wilderness of rocks; deep gorges, where the rivers are lost below cliffs and towers and pinnacles; and ten thousand strangely carved forms in every direction . . .

JOHN WESLEY POWELL, *The Exploration of the Colorado River and Its Canyons*, 1895

Monument Basin and the Island in the Sky, Canyonlands

MARK ZARN

Dust storm, Surprise Valley, The Maze, Canyonlands

and Colorado canyons before they meet, the high Island in the Sky mesa provides a perch for viewing the entire scene in one glance. Grandview Point, at the end of the good gravel road that reaches the southern tip of the Island, offers a view that rivals the Grand Canyon in scope.

The confluence of the Green and Colorado lies hidden in the tangle of canyons below you, but the serrated Needles are visible—on the east bank of the Colorado, halfway to the blue Abajo Mountains. The perfectly named Maze and Land of Standing Rocks cover the land on the west bank of the Green and Colorado. Immediately below you white-rimmed sandstone monoliths rise in the red alcove of Monument Basin.

A paved road leads into The Needles from the highway between Moab and Monticello. To reach The Maze country requires a dirt road adventure from near Hanksville on the west, an adventure that retraces Butch Cassidy's route into his remote canyon hideout, Robber's Roost. To penetrate to the rim of The Maze itself requires four-wheel-drive or backpacking. Slicing through Canyonlands are Labyrinth and Stillwater canyons on the Green, and Cataract on the Colorado below its confluence with the Green. These form another facet of the park experience, waters as wild as any left on the Plateau.

The Abajo Mountains stretch across the southern horizon at Canyonlands, streams flowing from their flanks through the Needles to the Colorado. Slip over the summit of the Abajos and drop southward and you'll find Natural Bridges National Monument tucked up against the south slope of the western ridges of the mountains.

A natural bridge spans a watercourse; an arch does not. This bit of information is one thing you may pick up on a visit to Natural Bridges. You'll also see three large natural bridges—all closely approached on a paved rim drive. To truly appreciate their size, however, walk the short trails that lead down into White Canyon and its tributaries and underneath each bridge.

Here you easily can see how such bridges form. Trace the course of White Canyon around meanders and picture floodwaters battering the walls at a sharp bend. Eventually a flood may pierce the thin inner curve of a loop, breaching the meander and taking the more direct route straight through. The roof of the hole gradually arches upward as floods widen the passage. New bridges are thick and massive, like Kachina Bridge; old bridges ready to fall are thin, graceful spans like Owachomo. The third of the Natural Bridges, Sipapu, demonstrates a bridge's middle age.

White Canyon winds down past Natural Bridges to meet the Colorado at Hite, where Glen Canyon on the Colorado officially begins. Upstream lies the rubbly country of Narrow and Cataract canyons. But downstream from Hite the Colorado winds its way through slickrock, through the peaceful miles that once formed Glen Canyon.

Today, Glen Canyon Dam has flooded most of Glen Canyon, creating a uniquely attractive reservoir but drowning the haunting beauty of the Colorado's mellowest canyon. Conservationists view this reservoir as a tragic, unnecessary mistake. They suggest that Lake Powell is probably a name whose honor John Wesley Powell would have preferred not to accept. The dam's defenders view it as a creator of valuable hydroelectric power and recreational opportunities.

The new recreation is motorized, however—powerboating and water skiing that can be had in many places. The reservoir ended an alternative recreational opportunity impossible to duplicate today: the chance to float the only *rapidless* Colorado River canyon. Inexperienced boaters could make the trip through Glen Canyon in small rafts, exploring side canyons without parallel on earth, canyons whose deep slots and amphitheaters formed cathedrals filled with magical reflected light.

The dam *has* provided easy access by boat to a huge section of back-country,

JOHN RUNNING

STEWART AITCHISON

Rainbow Bridge (top right)

Desert varnish, East Moody Canyon, Glen Canyon

though most motorboaters rarely walk more than a mile in from the lake. Huge tracts of this wilderness protected in Glen Canyon National Recreation Area can be reached and explored in solitude. The most famous remaining piece of Glen Canyon is the lower Escalante River, which preserves remarkable canyons that are only small-scale remnants of what was lost under the lake.

Up another side canyon lies Rainbow Bridge National Monument. Once so isolated it was a rare privilege to reach it, boats on Lake Powell now can reach Rainbow Bridge easily on a day's outing from Page, Arizona. Indeed, reservoir water backs up underneath the bridge itself, another of Glen Canyon's controversies. Even if the water does not weaken the bridge's foundations, some wonder if Rainbow Bridge, the sacred stone Rainbow Person of the Navajo, should receive such disrespectful treatment.

Rainbow Bridge is the world's largest known natural bridge, and arguably the most perfectly formed. Here the same processes that created the bridges at Natural Bridges operated on a grander scale to sculpt a symmetric red rock rainbow 275 feet long and 290 feet high. The bridge's setting adds to its impact, the curving stone set in a clean-walled slickrock maze draining from Navajo Mountain to the River.

Another extraordinary side canyon of Glen is that of Hall's Creek, which reaches far up into Capitol Reef National Park along the Waterpocket Fold. The Fold is one of several great bends in the flat-lying rocks of the Canyon Country, created by the pressures of regional uplift. This monocline steeply tilted the rocks in a long, narrow, flexed bank of formations bounded on either side by mesas and flat stacks of rock layers. Erosion has whittled at these upturned layers, eroding away the soft rocks, and leaving hard rocks standing high as barrier "reefs," rounded domes, fluted pinnacles.

Capitol Reef National Park outlines the Fold, from where it laps onto the High Plateaus at Thousand Lake Mountain south for almost a hundred miles to Glen Canyon. At the foot of Thousand Lake Mountain, the park includes two broad, arid valleys at the base of the Fold: South Desert and Cathedral Valley. The paved road (Utah Highway 24) cutting across the Reef along the Fremont River provides a single spectacular glimpse of the park. A good gravel road leads south along the west face of the Reef from the visitor center; a dirt road leads far south along the east side—well into the valley of Hall's Creek—connecting with the only other road crossing the Reef, the dirt Burr Trail from Boulder and Escalante, a wonderfully scenic approach to the park.

Throughout all these Canyon Country parks you see the characteristic landforms of flat sedimentary rocks in arid country. Hard layers resist erosion and cap mesas, protecting soft rocks below. Soft rocks often erode into badlands whose intricate networks of gullies skirt mesa bases. When a mesa erodes to a remnant no wider than it is high, it becomes a butte. Thin spires near the end of this cycle are called monuments. Just before monuments collapse, they form "balanced rocks." When tilted, the hard layers erode to standing ridges: hogbacks and reefs.

Gradual loss of blocks freed by release of internal pressures in the rock often forms great recesses—alcoves that may develop into arches and bridges. Arches often erode above seeps whose groundwater dissolves sandstone cement; natural bridges occur along drainages. Dry upland alcoves form the caves that shelter cliff dwellings. Floodwaters swirling rocks through a pothole above a cliff may grind right through, creating a horizontal pothole arch or bridge called a "potty."

The force behind all this erosion: water, water that you rarely see. Wind adds a touch here and there, and chemicals carried in water help to weather away stone. But the rivers and flooding arroyos and trickling seeps accomplish nearly all the erosional work on the Plateau—undercutting cliffs, washing away rockfall debris, grinding deeper into bedrock, and dissolving cement that binds together sand grains.

Each tributary feeds muddy floodwaters to the Colorado, which transports about three cubic *miles* of the Plateau downriver each year. Today, this load of debris clogs Lake Mead and Lake Powell, and eventually will fill them. Before the time of the dams, the River carried its burden all the way to the Gulf of California.

Time ticks slowly for the Canyon Country. A year means nothing, a human lifetime sees arroyos deepened a bit, the collapse of an arch or cliff here and there, the creation of a new window or two. A millenium scarcely changes the landscape.

Only in tens of thousands of years does the land see much change. And even then, a hundred thousand years is a fraction of an instant in the millions and billions of years of the earth's history. On this time scale the Plateau itself becomes a temporary phenomenon, a passing fancy of an earth with a restless skin of drifting, dynamic continents.

For now, though, the rivers and weather of the Canyon Country have yet to succeed in eroding the Plateau to plains. Our view, however fleeting a version of the scene it might seem to the earth, seems unchanging to us. We can return to the great cliffs of Capitol Reef or take the winding route up Salt Creek to Angel Arch in Canyonlands, and be fairly certain to find the scene unchanged since our last visit.

If you have limited time on this visit to the Canyon Country, tantalizing glimpses can be had from paved roads. Arches National Park and Colorado, Natural Bridges, and Black Canyon of the Gunnison national monuments all lend themselves to quick visits, with short walks leading to much of the best country in the parks. Capitol Reef and Canyonlands offer the combination of spectacular scenery along paved roads, with more remote country reached by gravel and dirt roads, and true wilderness reached only by hiking. Canyonlands contains an abundance of four-wheel-drive roads; many of Capitol Reef's back roads are passable to passenger cars. Boaters can head for Glen Canyon, a park also full of untouched back-country for hikers.

Whether you pass through quickly or stay a lifetime, the spirit of the canyons will leave its mark on you. Sun-baked rock, twisted juniper, pothole puddles teeming with fairy shrimp and tadpoles—these images ring with the power of beauty, the power of the desert. Treasure them as wild things must be treasured.

Remember them when you return home; someday the canyons will need your knowledgeable, friendly voice raised to help defend them.

Moonrise over the Waterpocket Fold and Henry Mountains, Capitol Reef (left)

Escalante Canyon, Lake Powell, Glen Canyon (right)

Sunrise from Bryce Point, Bryce Canyon

. . . the barricades of Bryce . . . the least overwhelming, dizzy, and least massive of the lot—but perhaps the most astounding . . . all suggestive of a child's fantasy of heaven . . .

THOMAS WOLFE, *A Western Journal*, 1938

THE HIGH PLATEAUS

Bryce Canyon National Park, Utah
Cedar Breaks National Monument, Utah
Zion National Park, Utah

LOOK WEST FROM THE CANYON COUNTRY and you look up; hazy blue, forested heights rim the horizon. Mountains, no doubt, beyond the Plateau?

Almost. These forested walls bordering the western Canyon Country rise to summits high enough to qualify as mountains—nine thousand to over eleven thousand feet high—but they have flat tops: still plateaus. Not just plateaus, but the High Plateaus.

The entire Plateau has undergone five to ten million years of uplift resulting in two miles worth of upward movement. But here at its northwest corner great blocks broken along faults ten million years earlier rose even higher, and probably still are rising. Three rows of these blocks, the High Plateaus, stretch from the Wasatch Mountains near Salt Lake City south to the Arizona-Utah line. The Paunsaugunt and Markagunt plateaus lie near the southern ends of two of these rows, great uplands whose Paiute names probably sound less familiar than the names of the canyons etched into their rims: Zion, Bryce, and Cedar Breaks.

The most distinctive High Plateau scenery exists in Bryce Canyon National Park and Cedar Breaks National Monument. Relatively young rocks cap these plateaus, rocks that have disappeared elsewhere in the region, stripped away long ago. This rock has its own personality—just as many others—but since it occurs in fully developed character only here, it defines a landscape unique on the Plateau.

Bryce Canyon preserves the archetype of this scene: rugged breaks, a fairyland of crumbling spires. More an amphitheater than a canyon, Bryce has been eroded into the east rim of the Paunsaugunt Plateau, where the plateau looks out over the Paria Valley two thousand feet below. No single river carved Bryce, but ten thousand rivulets draining the basin from the plateau rim to the Paria River, tiny streams, fed as much by snowmelt as by thundershowers. For Bryce's rim averages about eight thousand feet, with considerable snow falling during the long winter. Frost wedges apart spires on crackling cold nights; snow clothes the amphitheater, dissolving limestone and washing away a few more crucial layers of rock as it melts. Stand on the rim at Bryce on a warming winter morning and you can *hear* erosion, as melting pinnacles release countless small rockfalls.

The Silent City, Bryce Canyon

All pink, red, and white, the Wasatch Formation forms Bryce Canyon. These limestones and siltstones began as ooze at the bottom of lakes and shallow seas sixty million years ago. By the time these muds, long since transformed to rock, reached the surface again, freshly exposed by erosion, the pressures of uplift that raised the rock had also cracked it. As we know from the story of the fins at Arches, such cracked (jointed) rock is ready-made for destruction by the forces of erosion.

The spectacle of Bryce shows the results of this battle between attacking water and retreating limestone. The Silent City and the Fairyland, Queen Victoria and the Sinking Ship, Thor's Hammer and the Hindu Temples—these formation names give an inkling of the wondrous accomplishments of erosion here. Hard beds of sandstone and cemented gravel make protecting caps for pinnacles, but the limestone underneath eventually dissolves, and the pinnacles collapse. Meanwhile the canyons eat at the Paunsaugunt's rim, cutting back about one foot every fifty years.

Bryce's setting makes the fantasyland of red spires even more dramatic. The rim drive takes you to overlook after overlook perched on the edge of the Paunsaugunt. You look from the pink amphitheater in the foreground across the broad Paria River valley to plateaus towering over the Paunsaugunt—the Table Cliffs and Aquarius. The knife-edge of the Kaiparowits Plateau leads your eye south toward the Colorado River and the eighty-five-mile-distant blue dome of Navajo Mountain. And the bluest blue in sight: the arching, vibrant sky. Little wonder America reacted emotionally when in the 1970s proposals for a power plant on the Kaiparowits threatened the clarity of air that illuminates this scene.

Bryce reaches its peak of experience in these rim views. Wonderful short trails lead down into the breaks and connect to the twenty-eight-mile Under-the-Rim trail. The flat plateau summit invites a stroll through aromatic pines and firs, through meadows where you might catch a glimpse of a buck mule deer poised for flight or a soaring golden eagle. But Bryce hides little back-country. You'll get a good feel for the park even on a one-day visit.

Now travel west forty miles, across the Paunsaugunt Plateau, down into the Sevier River valley, and up again to the Markagunt Plateau—all the way to its western edge, just above Cedar City. Here you arrive at Cedar Breaks, and if you kept your eyes closed on the way from Bryce, when you reopened them you might accuse your driver of traveling in circles.

Before you, the familiar pink breaks eroded in the Wasatch Formation fill an amphitheater, though the details are a bit less intricately carved than Bryce. Views from the rim still carry your eye past pink cliffs to distant mountains—this time, ranges to the west in the Great Basin. You soon discover the most significant difference between Cedar Breaks and Bryce when you walk around a bit, and become winded almost immediately.

Cedar Breaks National Monument lies a full two thousand feet higher than Bryce, at about 10,400 feet. Just north of Cedar Breaks, Brianhead Peak reaches 11,315 feet. Bristlecone pines stand in twisted triumph on the rim of the breaks. Back from the windy cliff edge, on the summit of the Markagunt, not only do you find pine and aspen, spruce and fir, but alpine meadows luxuriant with wildflowers in summer. In fact, summer is not only the best time for Cedar Breaks meadow-romping, it is the only time when the visitor center is open and the road stays predictably clear of snow.

Southward, the Markagunt Plateau drops in great stair-step terraces toward the Grand Canyon country. Below Cedar Breaks the Virgin River begins, cutting across these plateau terraces on its way to the Colorado River. Where the Virgin cuts through the rim of the high Kolob Terrace, it drops steeply through a thick series of sedimentary rocks and carves a remarkable canyon: Zion.

Late fall in Zion Canyon (top)

Orderville Canyon, The Narrows, Zion (bottom)

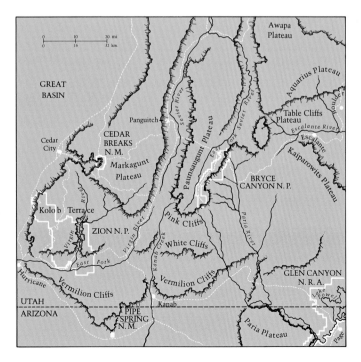

This geographic setting sounds similar to that of Bryce and Cedar Breaks. But two things set Zion apart: the *geologic* setting—older, different rocks—and the fact that here a permanent river slices *through* the rim rather than cutting at its edge from below with fingering headwaters.

Zion National Park preserves this great canyon and its upper terrace. The park also includes the Great West Canyon of North Creek and the "finger canyons" sliced through the Kolob Terrace northwest of the canyon of the Virgin. The canyons of Zion and the slickrock country around their rims come close to out-canyoning the Canyon Country itself. Similar landforms occur in both places (for the rock formations are the same), but Zion's higher rim gives it an overwhelming margin in scale.

The paved road up Zion Canyon pierces to within a mile of the Virgin River Narrows. In most of its drivable length, the canyon is about a quarter-mile wide and a half-mile deep. Huge blocks of bare Navajo Sandstone form the sheer cliffs of the upper canyon and the domes and temples of the rims. The sheer walls and smooth expanse of stone bring Yosemite Valley to mind, but Zion Canyon has seen no glaciers.

This Yosemite-in-sandstone owes its form to the downcutting Virgin River, the largest tributary to the Colorado in southwestern Utah. If the Virgin alone had created Zion Canyon, in uniformly hard rock, the entire length of the Canyon would be a deep slot like The Narrows, twenty feet wide and well over one thousand feet deep. The Narrows have been carved completely in fine-grained Navajo Sandstone, soft enough to yield to the river but hard enough to support the deep gorge without collapsing. The thirteen-mile Narrows hike from the top of the Markagunt Plateau to Zion Canyon ranks as one of the great canyon experiences of the entire Plateau.

Where the Virgin cuts through the base of the Navajo Sandstone, entering the shales of the Kayenta Formation, The Narrows cease and Zion Canyon begins. Here, as the river bared fresh rock in its slot, rain and frost weathered the newly-exposed soft rocks, and the sides caved in. The river immediately whisked away the debris, and slowly the canyon widened.

The undercut, higher cliffs of Navajo Sandstone collapse in huge slabs along joints. If joints parallel the direction of the canyon, smooth faces are left behind as each layer peels off, as on the Great White Throne. If joints intersect the canyon at right angles, the face of the receding cliff remains broken: fluted in gigantic columns.

At the rim of Zion Canyon, rounded domes and balds in the uppermost Navajo Sandstone characterize the long-eroded landscape. This horizontal exposure of sandstone erodes a grain at a time, with no undercutting streams and therefore no collapse of great blocks. The rounding temples and whalebacks create a landscape of almost as much variety in shape as Bryce, on a more monumental scale.

The Navajo is *sand* stone, huge piles of sand grains loosely cemented into rock. Before cementing, some 180 million years ago the sand grains piled in two-thousand-foot-deep dunes that covered nearly the entire Colorado Plateau, a desert perhaps similar in harshness and enormity to today's sand deserts in Saudi Arabia. As winds changed direction in this ancient land, they blew sand over dunes in layers at angles to the previous wind-deposited beds. These "bedding" layers at cross-angles to one another petrified with the rest of the dunes when the sea buried the Navajo desert after millions of years of drifting dunes and howling winds.

The sandstone we see today perfectly preserves these cross-bedded layers sweeping across the plane of the rock, creating delicate natural checkerboards where they intersect joints, as in famous Checkerboard Mesa at the park's east entrance, the easiest approach to this slickrock rim country. Zion owes much of its texture to this cross-bedded sandstone, the record of day-by-day weather changes in the time of the dinosaurs.

Sunset, Cedar Breaks

With permanent water in the Virgin River and many seeps and springs at the base of the water-transporting, porous Navajo Sandstone, Zion feels like paradise compared to some of the deep, dry canyons elsewhere on the Plateau. Waterfalls flow strongest during spring snowmelt, and, less predictably, after summer thunderstorms. Short trails in Zion Canyon lead to retreats like the Emerald Pools, Weeping Rock, and Hidden Canyon. Longer trails lead up to the west and east rims, where remarkable views down into Zion Canyon reward you for the steep climb.

Zion's wilderness contains enough side canyons for a lifetime of exploring. Two roads in addition to the Zion Canyon road provide access to the back-country: a short spur leading from Interstate 15 south of Cedar City into the Finger Canyons of the Kolob at the far northwest corner of the park, and a winding back road north from the town of Virgin through the high Kolob Terrace country in the center of the park.

These High Plateau landscapes come close to overwhelming the scenic rules of the Colorado Plateau. They *almost* pass for mountains, but lack the crucial abrupt summits. They *almost* manage to clothe themselves in green, but wherever water slices through to bedrock the resulting great canyons and amphitheaters give them away.

On the rims of Bryce or Cedar Breaks or Zion, no doubt exists. Though you may lean against a fir tree as you look out over the world, the colors and the light and the stone backbone of this world betray its identity: you could be nowhere but the Colorado Plateau.

Mule deer   HENRY SCHOCH
Claret cup cactus   DIANE ALLEN
Yuccas

Maidenhair fern in a hanging garden
Collared lizard
Gray fox   DIANE ALLEN

Interlude: THE BIOLOGICAL BOWL

AT THE BOTTOM OF THE BOWL lie low-elevation deserts, heat-shimmered canyons. At the rim of the bowl lie the High Plateaus, the mountains, cool, forested, high-elevation retreats.

The whole Plateau resembles such a bowl, dropping away from high elevations at its rim toward a center of bare slickrock and arid badlands. Temperature and precipitation determine where plants live, and where plants live largely determines where animals live. Crossing the Canyon Country and High Plateaus makes this dramatically evident.

In shale badlands and loose, sandy soils in low open areas, plants remain inconspicuous. The words "desert shrubs" bring to mind only sagebrush for many people, and sage indeed dominates the Great Basin Desert of Nevada and western Utah. But in most places here on the Plateau, the rocky soil is too harsh even for sage. Blackbrush, snakeweed, saltbush, greasewood—these plants form vast seas of gray across the canyon deserts, which receive only ten inches of precipitation or less.

Higher, where low hills retain a trace more moisture, the dwarf forest begins: piñon pine and juniper, stubborn, tenacious little trees that are perhaps the best living symbols of canyon landscapes. They grow singly from tiny cracks, on sheer cliffs, perched high on sandstone monuments. In places, piñon-juniper forest covers mile after mile with low trees—their gray-green *almost* coloring over the red earth. The drive from Blanding, Utah, to Natural Bridges National Monument brings with it sweeping views toward Monument Valley across dense piñon-juniper forest.

Higher up the side of the bowl, ponderosa pines appear—rare in most of the Canyon Country but dominant in the High Plateaus. On the High Plateau summits you reach the bowl's rim, and here the land feels like mountains, with forests of aspen, Douglas fir, spruce, and even bristlecone pine and alpine meadows, as at Cedar Breaks. Throughout these plant communities, diverse and characteristic plants grow between the dominant trees and shrubs: cactus and yucca, annual wildflowers, shrubs and small trees. A wet winter produces a display of spring flowers that plays glorious counterpoint to the colorful rocks.

Winding down the side of the bowl, permanent streams carry a group of water-loving plants far out into the desert. Fremont cottonwood, box elder, the introduced tamarisk—these streamside plants glow lime-green from miles away to draw desert wildlife in to water.

Perhaps the most magical of all the canyon plant worlds are cliffside hanging

Damselfly

Horsetails

MARK ZARN

gardens at springs and seeps. The contrast of these tangled gardens of greenery against their background of sterile slickrock and dusty shrubs makes them seem even lusher, though they pass for lush easily enough with fringes of maidenhair fern surrounding blossoming orchids, yellow and scarlet monkeyflowers, and columbines.

Animals, too, distinguish each level of the bowl. In the midday glare of a low canyon, you may see little movement: a collared lizard or antelope ground squirrel racing for shade, a jackrabbit stirred to flight by your presence—or by the silhouette of a coyote up on the mesa—a black-throated sparrow or canyon wren flitting toward a nest. And a raven or two glinting blue-black as they soar across a cloudless sky. Return at night and kangaroo rats bounce through the beam of your flashlight, the eyeshine of a tiny kit fox blinks back at you.

Move into piñon-juniper forest and mule deer move away ahead of you. Raucous piñon jays flap by, headed for a harvest of sweet piñon nuts. Ringtails hide in rocky side canyons. Night might bring a glimpse of a scampering piñon mouse, a bobcat, or even a wide-ranging cougar, with luck.

Up on the High Plateaus, summering deer and elk occur in abundance. Steller's jays and Clark's nutcrackers race chipmunks and golden-mantled ground squirrels for junk food handouts at overlooks. Meanwhile, violet-green swallows and white-throated swifts sweep by the cliffs below, ruffling the still air in their constant search for insects. In high meadows, yellow-bellied marmots—a sort of alpine woodchuck—whistle once before disappearing into their burrows. Nuthatches, chickadees, and juncos dart through the pines.

At pools, canyon tree frogs and Woodhouse toads chorus their mating fervor, a hymn to life, a song in praise of water. Some isolated springs at Zion and Capitol Reef contain snails found nowhere else. Dragonflies hover, water striders skim across the reflecting surface, beavers gnaw cottonwood and willow. Wait long enough at these water holes and you'll see most every canyon dweller come to drink, from desert bighorn to Gambel's quail, mourning dove to canyon mouse. And following them to the spring to hunt, gray fox and striped skunk, rattlesnake and red-tailed hawk.

Don't let the canyons and plateaus fool you: these badlands and deserts and bare slickrock domes are home to millions of animals, billions of plants. Down in the canyons, up on the high plateaus, out in the deserts, life thrives, flowers bloom, predators prey, seed-eaters scurry.

The great biological bowl of the Plateau is far from empty.

Rock squirrel in a singleleaf ash   *Indian paintbrush*

Petrified log, Blue Mesa

Here and there were fragments of petrified trees, all colours, some dull, some reflecting like marble, the many shades made brilliant by . . . the clear sunlight.
"Ei-yei! It is a place of jewels!"
OLIVER LA FARGE, *Laughing Boy*, 1929

THE PAINTED DESERT
Petrified Forest National Park, Arizona

IN PETRIFIED FOREST NATIONAL PARK the paradoxical nature of the Colorado Plateau stands out with special clarity.

The landscape feels simple. Great, sweeping plains, with sparse grass, lead into the distance toward a rim of wide horizons studded with far-off mountains and volcanic buttes. Low mesas capped by hard rock rise from the plain, and occasional violent rains create badlands cut in an intricate network of mounds and ridges and slopes between mesa tops and the flats below.

These badlands, colored every hue from scarlet to turquoise, form the Painted Desert. And strewn across this view—inconspicuous until you realize what they are—the forests of petrified logs lie scattered like bones, made of rock even more brilliant than the Painted Desert clays.

That's the simple side of the paradox—a flat desert grassland, a big sky, and the only trees (other than a few dwarf junipers, and some cottonwoods along the Puerco River) the old rock logs lying prone on the hillsides.

The complicated reverse of the paradox lies half-buried in this simple landscape: the story of *why* these logs are here. How did the greatest known concentration of petrified wood happen to occur here, of all possible spots on earth?

The answer: pure luck, geologic happenstance.

The rock layer that covers most of Petrified Forest National Park can be seen in many Plateau parks—the Chinle Formation. The Chinle is an easy layer to recognize, for its siltstones and mudstones and clays form badlands that glow with mineralized color: brick red, salmon pink, blue, brown, and every shade between. The great stretch of exposed Chinle that curves around the south edge of the Navajo Indian Reservation on the north bank of the Little Colorado River forms Arizona's Painted Desert. Petrified Forest National Park includes its eastern end.

These rocks formed from mud and silt carried in rivers and swamp waters two hundred million years ago. In and upstream from the swamps grew great coniferous trees, with amphibians and reptiles—and probably the first dinosaurs—wading through the muck of this marshy land.

As trees died, some washed into logjams in the muddy rivers of the area. Buried by mud, little oxygen could reach them to promote decay by microorganisms. The trees

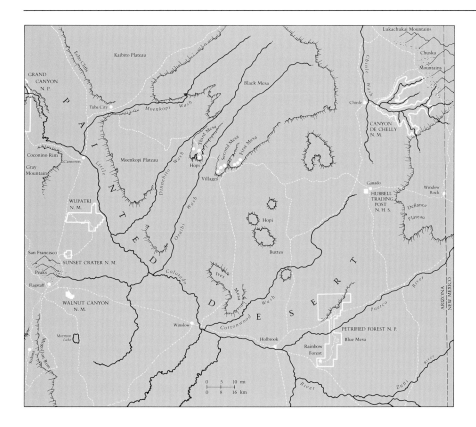

The Painted Desert from Lacey Point

lay encased in mud, soggy with water rich in dissolved silica. Slowly, silica crystals—called quartz, once crystallized—began to form in the tiny cells of the wood. Once started, the crystals grew ever larger, until a quartz crystal filled every cell in the tree.

In a process we still do not fully understand, entire logs eventually became "petrified," each bit of wood replaced with stone. Not every tree petrified with all details intact; many simply fossilized as a single massive crystal of quartz.

The probability of producing such a *concentration* of petrified wood, a concentration *visible* at the surface of the earth, is staggeringly small. For every organism that leaves a fossil of some bit of itself—wood, bone, or tooth—millions die and decay leaving no trace. Of the few living tissues which happen to fossilize, most lie buried where we can't see them. At Petrified Forest we see the only known fossilized forest of such luxuriance and beauty; here we have hit a once-in-an-eon jackpot.

Such rarity makes preservation of the area a crucial international concern. In the late 1800s, on completion of the railroad across northern Arizona, vandalism in the name of collecting reached a frightening peak. For not only is petrified wood abundant here, it is unusually colorful. Traces of minerals in the quartz turn logs red and yellow with iron pigments, blue-green with copper, and black with manganese. In the centers of some hollow logs, crystals could grow freely, producing gems of amethyst and rose and smoky quartz.

Early "collectors" took to dynamiting logs in search of such large crystals. When a mill opened nearby with plans to crush the logs into abrasives, concerned people realized they must act to protect Petrified Forest while something remained to protect. In 1906, protection arrived in the form of a national monument proclaimed by Theodore Roosevelt. Eventually, the monument was enlarged and Petrified Forest became a national park.

Today, as you rocket across the Navajo Country on Interstate 40 from Albuquerque to Flagstaff, an easy swing through Petrified Forest National Park allows you a close look at the great stone trees and the Painted Desert. The northern section of the drive follows the Painted Desert rim. To the south, the road passes through the famous stone forests: Rainbow, Jasper, and Crystal forests; the incredible jumble of logs and badlands at Blue Mesa; the arroyo-spanning log at Agate Bridge. The park has backcountry, too, in the Painted Desert wilderness.

Like all places, the longer you stay, the more you'll see. But here at Petrified Forest, if you take the time to appreciate the stone logs in their setting, you will understand why *every* piece of wood should remain here.

Willa Cather called this land "the floor of the sky," a floor paved with rainbows from summer storms, fallen to earth and turned to stone. This petrified wood surely belongs *here*—not in a museum or on a coffee table—for the people of the future to enjoy. Who knows what might result if we steal too many pieces of the floor of the sky?

. . . the desert . . . motionless and silent, it evokes in us an elusive hint of something unknown, unknowable, about to be revealed . . .

EDWARD ABBEY, *Desert Solitaire*, 1968

Winter moonrise, Blue Mesa

It seems a gigantic statement even for nature to make, all in one mighty stone word . . .

JOHN MUIR, *Steep Trails*, 1918

THE CANYON

Grand Canyon National Park, Arizona
Lake Mead National Recreation Area, Arizona

THE GRAND CANYON OF THE COLORADO forms the scenic climax of the Colorado Plateau. Here the forces that mold the rest of the Plateau exhaust their power, creating a canyon surpassing all others in proportion. The Grand Canyon overwhelms expectations based on the rest of the Plateau. At Zion Canyon, the scale is *big*, but the canyon is still recognizably a canyon.

Grand Canyon is more than a mere canyon, more than simply a geographic section of the Colorado Plateau. It is a mountain range in an abyss, a wildly baroque expansion on the essences of canyons, a world in itself. As geologist Clarence Dutton put it, ". . . the contrast between St. Mark's and the rude dwellings of the frontiersman is not greater than between the chasm of the Colorado and the trenches in the rocks which answer to the ordinary conception of cañon."

After carving the Grand Canyon—its last work on the Colorado Plateau—the Colorado River emerges into the desert, spent of its power. All its life seemingly taken from it by the last rapids of Lower Granite Gorge, the River leaves the wild Plateau where its red waters rule the land and enters the world of men. Even before the erection of a succession of dams below Grand Canyon, the River's emergence through the Grand Wash Cliffs decisively ended the Grand Canyon—and the Colorado Plateau. Today Lake Mead drowns the last forty miles of the River, but the canyon spirit survives still, right down to the final 279th mile of Grand Canyon.

Most visitors to Grand Canyon National Park first see the Canyon from the South Rim. The drive up from Flagstaff and Williams leads through soothing, rolling ponderosa pine forests, with open grassy parks allowing views of the San Francisco Peaks and Bill Williams Mountain. At the end of the road north, the rim of the Canyon suddenly appears, or more accurately, disappears! The mounting tension as you near the Canyon does nothing to prepare you for your first view; the North Rim rising on the horizon does nothing to warn you of what lies below it. Suddenly, you reach the edge of the Grand Canyon.

What makes this canyon "grander" than any other? The height of the plateaus the River cuts through provides much of the answer. Nowhere else on its course across the Colorado Plateau does such a high rim border the River. At its highest point, the

34

The River from Toroweap Overlook

nine-thousand-foot Kaibab Plateau towers six thousand two hundred feet above the River. The rock sequence also contributes to the grandness of the scene: a variety-pack of flat-lying sandstones, shales, limestones, siltstones, mudstones, granites, schists, and gneisses. Lastly, add the sheer power of the rasping River, as powerful here as anywhere on the Plateau.

Before dams controlled the Colorado above Grand Canyon, its waters ran from less than 1,000 cubic feet per second to a recorded high of 325,000 cubic feet per second. An average daily sediment load passing a gauge near Bright Angel Creek measured 500,000 tons suspended in the River, plus unmeasured additional tons of pebbles and boulders ground along the bottom. On a single day in 1927, 27,600,000 tons of sediment (that's twenty-seven and one-half *million* tons) passed the gauge!

The two ancient daily chores of the Colorado River, transporting Plateau debris to the sea and the resulting deepening of its channel, today occur in a puny facsimile of the figures of the previous paragraph. Glen Canyon Dam releases a controlled average flow of 12,200 cubic feet per second (sometimes less, rarely more). The rampaging, red Rio Colorado now runs with cold green water from the bottom of Lake Powell.

Yet the rapids still earn respect. The average drop of the River remains approximately twenty-five times greater than the Mississippi, most of the fall occurring in rapids where currents can reach twenty-five miles per hour.

So: the Colorado itself has the necessary power to account for the Canyon's depth, but how has it widened? We already know the answer: the same slow, erosive powers that work on every other Plateau landscape. Summer floods, snowmelt, frost-wedging, heat, cold, wind, chemical solution. Bit by bit, soft rocks weaken, hard cliffs are undercut and collapse, limestone dissolves. Floods roaring down side canyons wash debris to the big river below, and the Grand Canyon grows wider. Its width attests to its depth: side canyons owe their size to a constant attempt to keep erosional pace with the deeply cut master stream.

How long has the Colorado been at its work in the Grand Canyon? This question has perplexed every Plateau geologist since John Wesley Powell. It's particularly troublesome because it's an obvious question; it occurs to every curious park visitor. But the question still remains unanswered. Geologists know that the main uplift of the Kaibab Plateau is older than the River; they know the Colorado River downstream from western Grand Canyon is no older than eight or ten million years. Paradoxically, the Colorado River upstream from Grand Canyon is much older, perhaps thirty to forty million years old.

One theory suggests the younger river to the west gradually eroded the flanks of the Kaibab Plateau until it breached the uplift and captured the drainage of the older stream to the east, diverting the older stream's flow through what has become the Grand Canyon. Other theories suggest the ancient Colorado flowed off to the south from the Kaibab, through underground caves into the present Hualapai Indian country. The caves collapsed, forcing the river northwestward into its present drainage. Still another theory requires an antigravity waterfall to work! In short, no current theory marshals enough evidence to make it conclusive, but we do know much of the erosion in Grand Canyon has taken place recently, within the last ten million years, and that the Canyon was cut to within fifty feet of its present depth by three million years ago.

Today the River's course seems immutable, locked in an inner gorge of rock that carries it through four great canyons within the greater Grand Canyon. A river trip beginning at Lee's Ferry at the end of Glen Canyon first traverses Marble Gorge, named by the Powell expedition for the beautiful marble-like Redwall Limestone that characterizes the steep-walled canyon. Below Marble lies the Grand Canyon proper.

Here, the three Granite Gorges—Upper, Middle, and Lower—slice into dark, ancient metamorphic schist and gneiss, with great dikes of granite shot through the forbidding walls. Powell gloomily described these rapid-filled chutes as "our granite prision," yet still could marvel at the story told in the walls: "All about me are interesting geological records. The book is open and I can read as I run."

Above the Canyon lies a high green world of forested plateaus. The South Rim lies on the Coconino Plateau, which leads gently southward toward the San Francisco Peaks, and on to the Mogollon Rim where the edge of the Coconino Plateau marks the south edge of the Colorado Plateau, where the cliffs drop away to the desert highlands of central Arizona. Across from the Coconino at the deepest and widest part of the Canyon, the Kaibab Plateau towers fifteen hundred feet over the South Rim. Westward the Kaibab drops to lower platforms; the Kanab, Uinkaret, and Shivwits plateaus, respectively, rim Grand Canyon on the north all the way to the Grand Wash Cliffs bordering both the west edge of the Shivwits and the entire Colorado Plateau. On the South Rim west of the Coconino lies the Hualapai Plateau, also ending where the Grand Wash Cliffs plunge to the desert.

When you descend into the Canyon on any trail, you see not only a geological story in chapters, but a biological layering as well. Astounding moisture and temperature gradients between the rims and the Canyon floor create a series of constantly varying environments for living things. In the unusually moist winter of 1931–1932, the North Rim received seventeen and one-half feet of snow. Eleven miles away, the South Rim received just over eight feet, and at the bottom of the Canyon directly between these two points, no snow fell at all!

The Canyon encloses a reservoir of desert within its walls. Mesquite, ocotillo, catclaw acacia, agave, beavertail cactus—the true desert of the Inner Gorge allows

Deer Creek

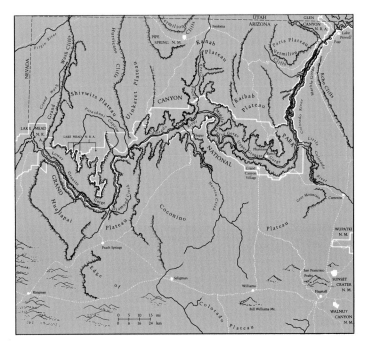

Mojave Desert plants to extend their range deep into the Plateau. A green jungle lines the riverbanks: tamarisk, cottonwood, and willow growing ever denser since the great cleansing floods ceased after construction of Glen Canyon Dam.

Above the Mojave Desert lie bands of desert scrub (dominated by blackbrush) and piñon-juniper–singleleaf ash woodland. Climbing out of the Canyon resembles a trip northward in latitude, every one-thousand-foot gain in elevation comparable to a three-hundred-mile leap in latitude. Up on the rims, ponderosa pines begin to replace piñon and juniper, and on the North Rim the cool, wet, high elevations support a spruce-fir forest highlighted with aspen groves, chattering red squirrels, and strutting wild turkeys.

The living symbol of the Canyon is surely the Kaibab squirrel. Like the similar Abert squirrel on the South Rim, the Kaibab squirrel relies almost completely on cones and sweet twigs of ponderosas for food. The Kaibab squirrel has a black belly and magnificent pure white tail, the Abert a white belly and a grayish tail; the Abert ranges widely over the Southwest, the Kaibab lives only in a 350-square-mile tract of pines on the North Rim.

Biologists guess that the ancestors of the Kaibab were Abert squirrels who extended their range across the Canyon in moister times, when ponderosas grew in the Canyon itself. When the climate warmed and ponderosas were restricted to the rims, the Kaibab population became isolated, and gradually evolved distinctive markings. Biologists currently class both squirrels as members of the same species, the tassel-eared squirrel. But they're not certain, and the Kaibab squirrels remain as isolated as ever on their North Rim home as confusion over their ancestry continues.

The Canyon has long been the scene of wildlife management controversies, perhaps because man has been attempting to "manage" this land longer than most desert

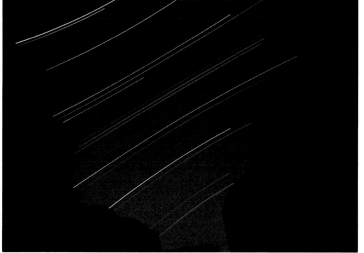

Star trails across the Canyon

JOHN RUNNING

The heavenly bodies look so much more remote from the bottom of a deep canyon than they do from the level. The climb of the walls helps out the eye, somehow. I lay down on a solitary rock that was like an island in the bottom of the valley, and looked up. . . . The arc of sky over the canyon was silvery blue . . . and presently stars shivered into it, like crystals dropped into perfectly clear water.

WILLA CATHER, *The Professor's House*, 1925

places and has had many opportunities to throw wrenches (though well-intentioned) in the ecological works of the Canyon. The Kaibab Plateau deer herd forms the first of these stories. In the late 1800s and early 1900s, the Kaibab became the scene of a massive predator control program, to "protect" livestock and deer. By 1930, the official predator kill read: 781 cougars, 554 bobcats, 4,889 coyotes, and 20 wolves.

The deer herd grew from 4,000 in 1906 to between 30,000 and 100,000 by 1924. Livestock had badly overgrazed the plateau in the 1800s, and the deer finished the job. Mass starvation followed, since the herd far exceeded the number the plateau could feed. They literally ate themselves out of a home.

Today, 10,000 deer survive, but wolves are extinct and cougars nearly so. Hunting outside the park boundary helps keep the herd in check by performing the duties of lost predators. Man has learned much about the crucial function of predators in natural communities since the days when Theodore Roosevelt went cougar hunting on the North Rim with the legendary guide Uncle Jim Owens.

The most recent controversy concerns wild burros, descended from prospectors' pack animals. These non-native grazers have seriously damaged Grand Canyon plant life. The National Park Service has encountered stiff opposition to its efforts to solve the problem by killing burros, and has yet to arrive at a humane solution that will save native Grand Canyon organisms from destruction.

Protection for the Grand Canyon has undergone a long odyssey. Declared a forest reserve in 1893, a game reserve in 1906, a national monument in 1908, and a national park in 1919, the central Canyon gradually acquired full protection. Later, the lower Grand Canyon and Marble Canyon upstream were declared national monuments, and finally the three areas were combined with parts of Lake Mead National Recreation Area in 1975 to form today's Grand Canyon National Park. The isolated north rim country along the Shivwits Plateau remains in Lake Mead National Recreation Area.

To *see* Grand Canyon requires only a quick trip to the South Rim, a trip made annually by some three million visitors. To *know* Grand Canyon requires somewhat more effort. Start by visiting the rims: the classic viewpoints along the South Rim, then the higher and wilder North Rim. A couple of hikes into the Canyon begin to increase awareness of its size: down the Bright Angel or Kaibab trails from the South Rim and across to the North Rim. Next try a little-used trail like the Hermit or Tanner, to feel the wild canyon in rugged solitary stillness. Walk down Havasu Creek to the land of the Havasupai Indians, where waterfalls and travertine terraces illustrate the meaning of their tribal name, the "People of the Blue-Green Water."

Run the River, almost three hundred miles of it. The surging current, the roar of rapids, the lush side canyons like Vasey's Paradise, Elve's Chasm, Deer Creek—see the River world, and the Canyon begins to make sense as a place, as a living, changing landscape.

But perhaps all you really need do is sit on the South Rim and watch. Watch the Canyon fill with light at dawn, watch summer afternoon thunderstorms boil through the world of stone, firing lightning bolts at the temples. Watch a Canyon sunset reduce the scene to an abstraction of orange and red, then lavender and mauve, with the tiny glint of the River a mile below. Return in winter to watch clouds fill the Canyon, snow blanket the cliffs.

And watch yourself change as these views enter your memory; let wilderness rejuvenate your soul, listen to time tick in the earth's heart and remember humility. Watch the Grand Canyon and see anything and everything contained in the earth and in yourself.

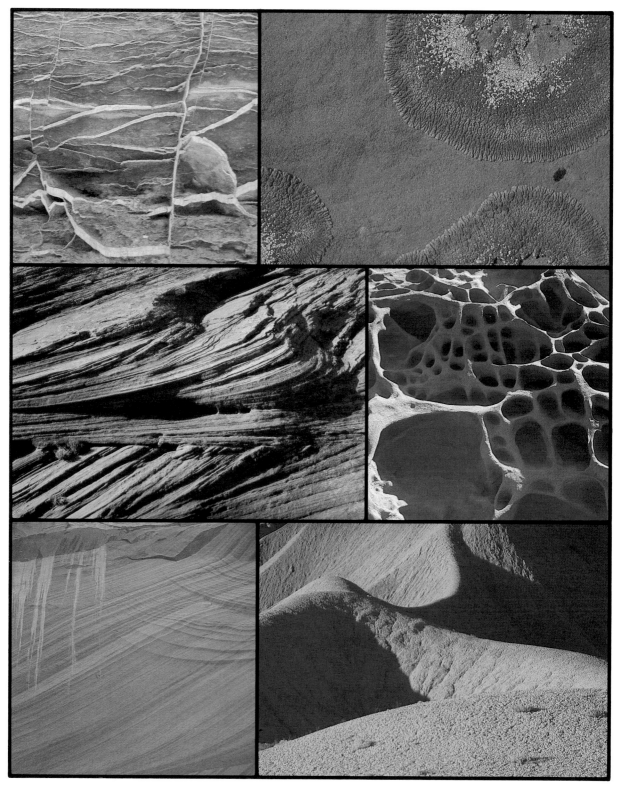

Gypsum layers, Carmel Formation
Cross-bedding, De Chelly Sandstone
Alkali and cross-bedding, Navajo Sandstone

Lichens, Entrada Sandstone
Honeycombing, Wingate Sandstone
Badlands, Mancos Shale

Interlude: THE GRAND STAIRCASE

FROM THE BOTTOM OF THE GRAND CANYON to the rim of Bryce and Cedar Breaks, two billion years of earth history have been exposed by the last few million years of erosion. The rocks are old; the landscape is young. Two dozen formations make up this great stack of rock—mostly sedimentary rocks.

How do we sort out the names and ages of all these rocks if we aren't geologists? The Kayenta Formation, middle formation of the Glen Canyon Group, is mostly stream deposits, containing dinosaur fossils and tracks, Mesozoic (late Triassic), about 170 million years old. Not much help unless you use these technical words often enough for them to have instant meaning.

To truly understand ancient rocks like the Vishnu Schist at the bottom of the Grand Canyon is close to impossible. Such rock formed 1.7 *billion* years ago from sediments laid down *two* billion years ago.

A billion, a million, a thousand—these numbers seem so great to us who count our years in decades. Feeling the age of the earth and its rock layers comes hard. Perhaps the easiest way to become familiar with Plateau rocks is simply to make friends with each one as it comes your way. Most have distinctive personalities, and the *most* distinctive give you anchor points in the stack which you can recognize everywhere.

Walk out of the Grand Canyon and you walk up through the oldest Plateau rocks, those from the long first and second eras of earth history. About a mile's worth of rock layers pass under your feet: the broad Tonto Platform of the Bright Angel Shale, the towering cliffs of the Redwall. Most of these rocks are not as widespread on the Plateau as younger layers; in most places erosion hasn't cut deep enough to expose them.

Walk north toward Zion and you ascend the famous Grand Staircase of southern Utah. Here you meet rocks you'll see all over the Plateau. Sedimentary rock layers in this region tilt gently down to the north, so as you travel north the formations pass in review—the hard layers standing high as cliffs, the soft ones as broad slopes and valleys.

As you leave the flat surface of the Kaibab Limestone on the Kaibab Plateau, you must cross the rubbly ledges of the Chocolate Cliffs (Moenkopi Formation) and the great red barrier wall of the Vermilion Cliffs (Moenave, Kayenta, and lower reddish Navajo) before you reach the White Cliffs of Zion's Navajo Sandstone. Zion Canyon itself slices through the entire thirty-five-hundred-foot stack of rocks from the earth's third, or middle era, from Navajo right down to the Kaibab Limestone that capped the Grand Canyon and ended the story there.

Beyond, on up past the Gray Cliffs separating the Kolob Terrace from the upper Markagunt Plateau, you finally arrive at the Pink Cliffs (Wasatch Formation) of the fourth, and present, geologic era—quite young rocks compared to the old, stony depths of the Grand Canyon. The last two stair-steps took you through another two thousand feet of rock—crowning two miles of rock formations since you left the Colorado River at the bottom of Grand Canyon.

Some of these formations should be old friends: the cross-bedded domes of white, pink, and golden Navajo Sandstone are unmistakable, forming the rim of Zion Canyon, the summit of the Waterpocket Fold at Capitol Reef, the arch of Rainbow Bridge, most of Glen Canyon, and seen as far east as Arches and north to Dinosaur.

The colorful badlands of Chinle Shale turn up again and again: in the Painted Desert at Petrified Forest, and at the base of the great cliffs at Zion, Capitol Reef, and over into Canyonlands. Gray badlands mean Mancos Shale, which forms huge mesas capped by Mesa Verde Sandstone at Capitol Reef, Dinosaur, and Mesa Verde, and the long line of the Book Cliffs on the northern horizon at Arches and Colorado National Monument.

*Geology here forever dominates life and gives it its
ultimate meaning.*

FRANK WATERS, *The Colorado,* 1946

Cedar Mesa Sandstone, The Needles, Canyonlands

Other formations occur eastward. In the Canyon Country, Wingate Sandstone
supports the white Navajo domes on fluted red columns. These steep Wingate cliffs
form the great face of Capitol Reef and guard the basins of Canyonlands with author-
ity; only the dedicated traveler manages to find routes over them. A couple of layers
below the Wingate lies another layer of massive sandstone—the Cedar Mesa Member
of the Cutler Formation. Cedar Mesa Sandstone forms The Needles and The Maze in
Canyonlands, and all three bridges at Natural Bridges have been carved from this
wonderfully white-and-red banded rock.

Within each formation, incredible variation in texture occurs. The strength of
cement varies, and as water trickles through sandstone, it dissolves the weakest
cement first, honeycombing cliffs. Entrada Sandstone at Capitol Reef forms crumbly
mudstone monuments in Cathedral Valley; the same formation stands as massive,
cross-bedded sandstone in the fins of Arches and the cliff walls at Colorado.

The smallest variant results in unique erosional forms—a bit of mudstone here, a
limy shelf there, a hard lens of sandstone sandwiched between soft layers, black dikes
of volcanic rock. Given three dozen kinds of Plateau rocks, deposited over two billion
years of time across 130,000 square miles, uplifted, and then whittled at by ten million
frosty winters, ten million windy springs, ten million summers of flash floods, the
possible results in rock shapes are infinite.

Every canyon holds in trust secret sculptures, unique details indifferent to discovery and appreciation, slowly eroding to dust and clay and sand. Black mineral stains of
desert varnish and the colorful scaly growth of lichens overlay the sculptured rock
with yet another infinitely variable element.

Red rock country may look monotonous to some. For others, sensing the variety in
rocks can leave them close to exhaustion. This same exhaustion comes at the end of
an afternoon in a good art museum: satiation of eye, saturation of the aesthetic spirit.

Here, though, the museum has a constantly rotating exhibit. Every year the pictures
change, the sculptures evolve, the styles progress.

If only we could return again in two million years . . .

Sunrise, Lomaki Ruin, Wupatki

Part Two: THE OLD ONES

'From the ancient dwelling there came
always a dignified, unobtrusive sadness; now stronger, now fainter—
like the aromatic smell which the dwarf cedars gave out in the sun—but always
present, a part of the air one breathed. . . . that peculiar sadness—a voice out of
the past, not very loud, . . . went on saying a few simple things to the solitude
eternally

WILLA CATHER, *The Song of the Lark*, 1915

44

Keet Seel, Navajo National Monument

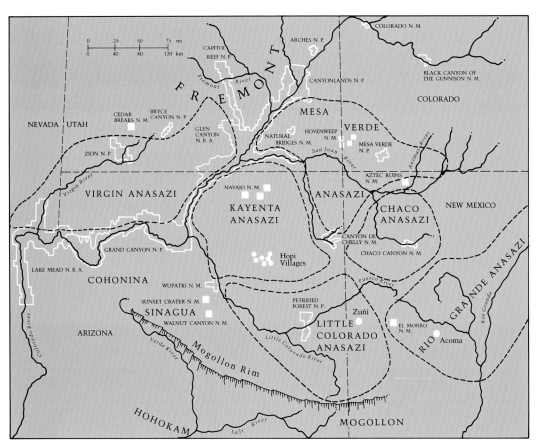

Newspaper Rock, Petrified Forest

. . . the Anasazi . . . were slightly shorter than the average today, had straight black hair and spoke in tongues unintelligible to the western ear. They were people worried about their crops and children, remembering the past and wondering about the future.

J. RICHARD AMBLER, *The Anasazi*, 1977

ANASAZI

Chaco Canyon National Monument, New Mexico
Mesa Verde National Park, Colorado
Navajo National Monument, Arizona
Canyon de Chelly National Monument, Arizona
Aztec Ruins National Monument, New Mexico
Hovenweep National Monument, Utah/Colorado
Canyonlands National Park, Utah
Natural Bridges National Monument, Utah
Petrified Forest National Park, Arizona
Glen Canyon National Recreation Area, Utah/Arizona

IN CANYONS AND ON MESA TOPS through the Four Corners region, the cliffrock does not always form monuments to geologic processes alone. Here and there, stones have been shaped and fitted and mortared. Alcoves shelter crumbling rock houses built seven hundred or more years ago—monuments to man and the power of humans to shape the land, to design and craft and invent, to create civilizations from rock and wood, from hard work and clever thinking. But then to leave, for these stone walls lie silent, their builders gone.

Though the cliff dwellings of the past lie empty, their spirit lives still in the modern Pueblo Indians, whose ancestors built the ruined stone cities. When the Pueblo's modern adversaries, the Navajo Indians, arrived in the Southwest after 1500, they called the builders of these old cities the Anasazi. This Navajo word today translates roughly as "The Ancient Ones," but originally meant "Enemy Ancestors."

Archaeologists divide the Anasazi into two primary cultural stages, the earlier Basketmakers, and the later Pueblos, who gradually developed into the modern Pueblo Indians. To understand the Anasazi heritage, we must start long before even the Basketmakers, at the very beginning of Southwest prehistory.

Man probably arrived in the Southwest by about thirteen thousand years ago. These earliest Southwesterners adapted to a decrease in numbers of game animals and to a climate turning more desert-like by concentrating less on big game hunting and more on the collecting of wild food plants to make their living. To the east, native peoples on the Great Plains remained hunters right up to the buffalo Indians of historic times. But by at least five thousand years ago, the desert people began to place major

SHERRY MANGUM

Pueblo Bonito, Chaco Canyon

A "hallway" and
  a dozen kivas

SHERRY MANGUM

emphasis on plant foods. Grinding stones became more important than spear points.

By 2000 B.C. corn evidently had made its way northward to the Southwest from the Mexican heartland, where the golden-kerneled plant was domesticated. At first, people would plant a plot of corn and leave it to its fate while they retraced traditional gathering routes. They treated corn just as they did wild food plants: if they returned to find mature ears, they harvested grain raised almost effortlessly. If the crop failed, they simply fell back on old reliables like piñon nuts and Indian ricegrass seeds.

Gradually, wanderers invested more effort in their corn, tending it through summer, protecting it from insects and other hungry animals. Once their storage bins filled after a couple of good years, trusting to their fields for food began to pay off. The necessity to be near their corn brought a new way of life: no longer constantly on the move, people could build permanent homes, planting cultural roots.

By about the the time of Christ, different peoples living in different places had adapted differently to the incredible range of Southwestern environments. Quite naturally, once the wanderers stayed put, the land of each began to shape their cultures. Mountain, desert, and plateau cultures took separate paths from here on.

Mountain people took the first strides toward village life. In the rugged highlands of central Arizona and New Mexico wedged between the northern Plateau and southern deserts, the Mogollon culture slowly took shape. These people created the first pottery in the Southwest, and even in their early years lived in villages of partially buried pit houses roofed with wood covered with earth, with large structures in each settlement evidently of special ceremonial nature. At about the same time, a desert culture developed in southern Arizona, the Hohokam, or "Old Ones" to the modern Pima Indians. By A.D. 300, the Hohokam were employing extensive irrigation agriculture.

The Plateau people had begun this same transition from gathering and collecting to agriculture, but much more slowly. During the first five centuries of the Christian era they added corn and squash agriculture to their extensive gathering and hunting. They used the atlatl (spear-thrower) to extend the range and power of their spears, but lacked the bow and arrow. Some of these people lived in caves, building only slab-lined storage pits, while others began to live in pit houses.

Before you judge these early Anasazi as unbearably primitive, consider some of their other accomplishments. Their finest sandals were woven from plant-fiber string (made mostly of yucca and apocynum, a type of milkweed). These sandals had from fifteen to thirty-six cord warps along the length of the sandals, with more strings woven tightly across them; one pair used twelve hundred feet of string for the ties alone. Later versions had raised designs on the soles and colored designs woven in. Flexible bags also were woven from fiber string. And then there are the baskets . . .

These Anasazi have a name that memorializes their power to weave art from leaves and stems and twigs: the Basketmakers. They made baskets ranging from a few inches to several feet in diameter, and wove some tightly enough to hold water. Since they had no pottery, they cooked in these baskets, parching seeds by shaking them in shallow trays with hot coals, cooking in basketry bowls by dropping in hot stones to boil the liquid contents.

The Basketmaker Anasazi reached their cultural peak between A.D. 500 and 700. Baskets, sandals, and string bags had leveled off at a plateau of high artistry, and more permanent villages of pit houses became the normal living arrangement. Several new additions to their culture moved them rapidly forward: beans were added to the crops grown, pottery became common (indeed, necessary, if those beans were to be boiled!) and cotton appeared. These discoveries, surely exciting to the Basketmakers, came from the south, probably via Mogollon people who had used such things for centuries. The bow and arrow arrived about this same time, probably from the north.

At about this time, too, a new fashion in physical appearance suddenly appeared, a fashion that defines the Basketmaker/Pueblo transition. After A.D. 700, Anasazi mothers began strapping their babies to hard wooden cradleboards instead of using the traditional padded cradles. In doing so, they permanently flattened the backs of their babies' heads. No one knows for sure why these normally long-headed people took to this custom, but they continued to deform their children's heads in the centuries that followed while their culture blossomed.

The Anasazi culture is a continuum, and late Basketmakers and early Pueblos surely viewed themselves as members of the same people. But archaeologists arbitrarily have chosen this time in Anasazi history as a dividing point—between cultural stages, not between different people.

By A.D. 1000, Pueblo people lived from the Rio Grande to eastern Nevada in thousands of small villages (most with three to twenty living rooms), and some large masonry pueblos. As surface pueblos became common, the old, half-subterranean pit house evolved into the kiva, the underground ceremonial chamber still used by modern Pueblo Indians.

By this time, Anasazi depended on agriculture for much of their food. Their pottery was distinctive: plain gray-white cookware corrugated on the outside with unsmoothed coils pinched with regular thumb-nail indentations, and white pottery decorated with beautiful geometric patterns in black. Anasazi must have felt an extraordinary vitality in these years of expansion and cultural development. Now they had no need to borrow ideas from their Mogollon neighbors. Instead, the Mogollon began borrowing from their former country cousins, the Anasazi.

The years from about 1100 to 1300 saw full flowering of the trends of the development years. Masonry pueblos grew larger and larger, growing to small cities of hundreds of rooms and several stories. Not only architecture, but pottery, jewelry, and other arts reached new heights. Trade flourished between Anasazi groups and with distant cultures; prized articles obtained from the latter included shell ornaments, copper bells, and macaws. This stage marked the full maturity of the Anasazi, the Great or Classic Pueblo period.

Events then moved rapidly—just as the pace of history in our own culture has increased with technological growth. Not long after the great pueblos rose on the mesa tops, the people abruptly abandoned them and retreated to the damp, dark caves where most Anasazi had not lived since Basketmaker times. Perhaps raids by nomadic tribes forced the move. New pueblos rose in the caves, and it is these last homes (preserved in their alcoves over the centuries while exposed mesa-top pueblos disintegrated) that today give us our most spectacular image of the Anasazi.

Then, starting in the 1100s and reaching the stage of mass exodus in the 1200s, the people began abandoning their homeland. Drought, arroyo cutting, and overuse of resources like timber and soil had created insurmountable problems, perhaps compounded by raiders who, if they existed, must have delighted in plundering and burning precious Anasazi cornfields. The Anasazi moved south and east, leaving the entire San Juan River drainage by 1300. They drifted slowly through the mountain country of central Arizona and New Mexico and eventually concentrated in the few locations where Pueblo people live today: the Hopi and Zuñi villages in the Little Colorado River drainage and the series of pueblos along the Rio Grande.

The Anasazi heartland was the San Juan River basin, immediately surrounding modern Four Corners. Here the Basketmakers hollowed out their first pit houses to begin the long road toward the time of the Great Pueblos. Gradually, distinct regional variations emerged. These branches began to acquire unique personalities as masonry and pottery styles took different directions in different areas, and by A.D. 900, conspicuous cultural variation had developed.

Chaco Canyon led the way in these early days. In this narrow strip of irrigable land stretching twenty miles along Chaco Wash in a rather desolate section of northwestern New Mexico, the Anasazi first reached the climactic stage of great masonry pueblos. By the late 11th century, thirteen multistoried pueblos prospered along the canyon floor, each a small city of remarkable complexity. Dozens of five to twenty room pueblos filled in the gaps along the base of the cliffs and up on the mesas, bringing the total population for Chaco to about seven thousand people.

To feed these crowds, Anasazi farmers must have supplemented crops grown along Chaco Wash with food imported from the San Juan country. An extensive road system visible today preserves the probable routes taken by such supply expeditions.

Religion surely played a major role in the lives of Chacoans. Not only are clan kivas abundant, but several "great kivas" flourished here, elaborate circular structures epitomized by Casa Rinconada, sixty-four feet in diameter. Large numbers of people must have witnessed the great kiva ceremonies, including women as well as the men who used the clan kivas almost exclusively. Arts flourished, too: Chacoans were the master jewelers and ornament carvers of the Anasazi.

The greatest of Chaco's towns was—and is—Pueblo Bonito, probably the largest prehistoric community in the Southwest. Begun in the 900s with the final D-shaped floor plan already evident, for 150 years Chacoans added to the great structure. When finished, Bonito contained 800 rooms reaching to 4 and 5 stories. Masonry techniques reached an artistic peak here unmatched elsewhere by the Anasazi.

'The tower was the fine thing that held all the jumble of houses together and made them mean something. . . . In sunlight it was the colour of winter oak-leaves. . . . It was more like sculpture than anything else . . . preserved in the dry air and almost perpetual sunlight like a fly in amber, guarded by the cliffs . . .

WILLA CATHER, *The Professor's House,* 1925

MARC GAEDE

Square Tower House, Mesa Verde (left)

The Cliff Palace, Mesa Verde (right)

SHERRY MANGUM

In Pueblo Bonito and the other great Chaco Canyon pueblos, the Anasazi built massive walls in three layers: an outer and inner facing of carefully shaped sandstone slabs in decorative bands, and an interior rubble filling. Then, after such careful masonry work, they covered the banded facade with plaster!

Chaco's golden age passed quickly. The remarkable concentration of people could only last while their fields produced at peak capacity. When arroyos began to trench the valley floor and wash away soil, ruining croplands and destroying irrigation systems, Chacoans could do nothing but abandon the great pueblos and move away. Centuries of tree-cutting upstream had destroyed the watershed, and unimpeded run-off initiated this disastrous arroyo-cutting. Only a few people remained in Chaco Canyon after 1200.

Meanwhile, other Anasazi to the north had finally begun the transition to semi-urban living made so early at Chaco. Long an Anasazi home, an isolated high mesa in southwestern Colorado known today as Mesa Verde (Spanish for "green tableland") saw the second great Anasazi cultural boom, beginning about 1100. Large mesa-top pueblos began to replace the hundreds of tiny settlements tucked away on the mesa. Some, like Farview Pueblo, grew as high as four stories, by piecemeal addition rather than planned design. Kivas, originally out in front of the main dwellings, became enclosed within pueblo walls. Masonry was distinctive and superb: Mesa Verde craftsmen pecked rocks to size and built thin walls with little mortar and no rubble fill.

Mesa Verdeans may have been harrassed by raiders more than Chacoans. Round and square towers, possibly for defense, characterized these new pueblos. And after only a hundred years in the large mesa-top communities, the Mesa Verde people abruptly moved again—to the caves under the cliffs. Though south-facing caves provided protection from winter storms, they made crowded spaces for building. The Anasazi may have made this move primarily for defense.

Sunset on the towers, Hovenweep

Even in the caves, great pueblos grew from the rock. Cliff Palace, the largest Anasazi cliff dwelling, contained 200 rooms and 23 kivas. Already on the downswing from glory days on the mesa top, an unrelenting drought from 1276 to 1299 evidently proved the last straw for Mesa Verde culture. Anasazi streamed south, leaving Mesa Verde abandoned by 1300.

The third great focus of Anasazi civilization grew in the rugged canyon country near Navajo Mountain, in northeastern Arizona. These people take their name from the nearby modern Navajo town: we call them the Kayenta Anasazi. Kayenta people lived in a harsh land, where hard work resulted in small harvests. The Kayenta never enjoyed the abundance of leisure time that enabled the arts of Chaco Canyon and Mesa Verde to flourish. Kayenta masons never gloried in their craft as the eastern groups did. They continued to use wattle-and-daub (mud plastered over woven sticks) along with masonry, and lived in pit houses right up to Classic Pueblo times, building them at the same time and immediately adjacent to masonry cliff dwellings. Kivas occur in fewer numbers than at either Chaco or Mesa Verde.

Even so, the Kayenta made fine pottery: intricate black-on-white and the first popular Anasazi polychrome (black, white, and red on orange). At their peak, the Kayenta concentrated in the area surrounding Tsegi Canyon. Betatakin and Keet Seel pueblos in the Tsegi and Inscription House to the west were among the last villages to be abandoned in the San Juan drainage. These three great pueblos are preserved today in Navajo National Monument; a paved road leads to the rim above the magnificent alcove sheltering Betatakin.

These three areas formed the core of Anasazi tradition. But Anasazi ruins are by no

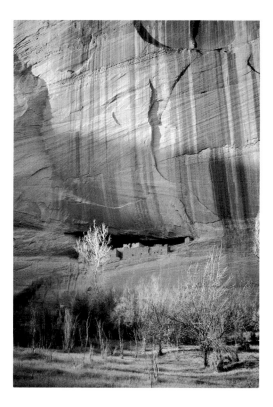

SHERRY MANGUM

means confined to Mesa Verde National Park and Chaco Canyon and Navajo national monuments. Throughout the Four Corners country, any patch of plantable alluvium with a living site and water close at hand seems to yield crumbling granaries and a few pot sherds on close inspection. Anasazi lived as far west as Zion and Grand Canyon and north to what is now Glen Canyon National Recreation Area and Canyonlands National Park. Many ruins and much rock art preserve their lifeway in remote corners of Canyonlands. Natural Bridges National Monument also contains fine ruins. And at Hovenweep National Monument, at the heads of small canyons on the Utah-Colorado border, Anasazi of the Mesa Verde culture built fortified pueblos in the 1200s, with many well-constructed square, oval, circular, and D-shaped towers, today accessible by good dirt road.

Aztec Ruins National Monument, near Aztec, New Mexico (and with no connection to the Aztecs of Mexico!), contains a 500-room surface pueblo where Anasazi lived and irrigated fields along the Animas River. Aztec lies about halfway between Mesa Verde and Chaco Canyon, and, predictably, both great cultures influenced life at Aztec. Chaco influence gradually decreased as Chaco culture waned and Mesa Verde culture blossomed. While Chaco still dominated the region, the Aztec Anasazi built a great kiva. Excavated and restored in 1934, today this great kiva gives a wonderful impression of how Anasazi masonry must have looked when uncrumbled and newly plastered.

A southern frontier of Anasazi influence lies today within Petrified Forest National Park. Basketmaker sites show Anasazi were here by A.D. 300. Later, masonry pueblos were built, some small pueblos crafted entirely from jewel-like chunks of petrified

Small ruin, Davis Canyon, Canyonlands

DAVID JOHNSON

The Anasazi . . . did not simply walk out into the sands . . . and disappear, vaporizing like the morning dew. . . . they . . . would never really vanish because they are a part of the genetic and mythic memory of men yet building pueblos of stone and adobe, women still shaping their pottery, and young boys learning their way into manhood in the kivas.

DONALD G. PIKE, *Anasazi: Ancient People of the Rock,* 1974

wood. The park contains a remarkable wealth of rock art. And the story of the great exodus southward is told by the 125-room Puerco Ruin, built by late Anasazi farming the Puerco River bottomlands, and inhabited to around 1400, when the Puerco Anasazi moved on, too.

Lastly, Canyon de Chelly National Monument preserves small ruins in a spectacular canyon. Single caves here demonstrate the entire span of Anasazi history, from Basketmaker to Classic Pueblo, lived out in one spot. Mummy Cave in the branch canyon of Del Muerto shows this long span. And White House Ruin, its plaster gleaming still after 700 years, serves as one of the classic images of the Anasazi. Canyon de Chelly is a narrow, deep, steep-walled canyon, and White House perches in a cave at the base of a 500-foot tapestried wall—a glorious sight and surely a glorious place to have lived. Today, Navajo Indians live in the Canyon, and to travel into the canyons anywhere but along the rims or to White House requires an authorized guide.

Indian ruins in the Southwest still means Mesa Verde to most people. And no one should miss this monument to Anasazi skill. The great cliff dwellings of Mesa Verde are unforgettably flavored with the spirit of their creators, for no other people ever lived on the mesa. It is still the land of the Anasazi, and no one else.

But Mesa Verde has become so widely known that in summer crowded ruins and heavy traffic on the rim drives sometimes overwhelm the spirit of the canyons. Take the time to go elsewhere, too. Visit a pueblo where you can sit alone for an afternoon and imagine the Anasazi chatter from the plaza, where corn cobs and pot sherds still litter the ground around the ruins. Walk the six-and-one-half miles to Keet Seel in Navajo National Monument, or drive the isolated dirt road into Chaco Canyon on a crisp fall day, or wander the Canyonlands back-country. Here you feel the tingle of discovery, never knowing quite when you'll spot, hidden in a recess, a cryptic petroglyph or a granary with its door still in place. Some ruins seem so fresh, so intact that you find yourself looking for growing corn and bean plants in the streambed below.

In such places you almost can convince yourself that in some remote canyon the Anasazi lifeway continues.

Clouds, black sand, and snow, Sunset Crater

It is a desolate, nightmarishly beautiful scene of unearthly desolation and of desolation which looks so newly wrecked that one almost expects to see the lava still smoking.

JOSEPH WOOD KRUTCH, *Grand Canyon: Today and All Its Yesterdays*, 1958

SINAGUA

Sunset Crater National Monument, Arizona
Wupatki National Monument, Arizona
Walnut Canyon National Monument, Arizona

NEAR THE SOUTHERN EDGE of the Colorado Plateau, the San Francisco Peaks pierce the sky in a graceful silhouette that forms a landmark for 150 miles around. The highest point in Arizona, the glaciated, volcanic 12,670-foot Peaks are sacred to both the Hopi and Navajo. These mountains are not only prominent in today's landscape but in the landscapes of tribal legend.

After two million years of volcanic activity, the 400 cinder cones surrounding the Peaks have formed numerous lava flows that cap mesas and dam creeks, while cinders form massive black sand dunes. The most recent of these cinder cones erupted in the winter of 1064–1065, to permanently transfigure not only the land but the lives of the Sinagua Indians then living there.

When the earth stirred at this volcano we call Sunset Crater, the Sinagua surely gained new respect for the power of the mountains and cinder hills which usually loomed benignly over their homeland. Breaking the years of calm, the land shivered and shook with the tremors of earthquakes as a crack opened in the ground and molten rock began pouring out over the land. Lava sprayed from the fissure under tremendous pressure, tiny molten droplets hardening in the air to form cinders, and then raining down in great heaps around the vent. Larger globs of lava hardened in streamlined balls called volcanic bombs.

Lava continued to pour forth for months. Under a sky black with ash, two major lava flows ceased their incandescent steaming and hardened into rivers of naked black rock. The belching, smoking cone grew until its cinders piled 1,000 feet high. Winds spread ash and cinders from Sunset Crater over the surrounding 800 square miles; this dark curtain disrupted the local climate and may have caused such normally dependable food sources as piñon to fail.

Then, gradually, the eruption slowed to a sputter of gaseous vapor, adding a last touch to the new volcano by staining cinders at the crater rim with red iron oxide. Eight hundred years later John Wesley Powell named Sunset Crater for these red cinders that brighten the black volcano in a colorful illusion of last light even in midday sun.

The Sinagua had been living at the base of the Peaks for 500 years when Sunset Crater rocked their world. In fact, we can pinpoint the date of eruption by dating timbers from their pit houses buried by volcanic ash. These people owe their modern name, Spanish for "without water," to the rarity of surface water in their homeland. To live here as sedentary dry-land farmers took ingenuity and skill.

Early Sinagua began to build permanent timber, mud, and stone houses and grow corn about A.D. 600, gradually abandoning their nomadic life of hunting and gathering. They had neighbors on all sides with whom to trade goods and ideas: the Kayenta Anasazi to the northeast, the unsophisticated Cohonina to the west, master-irrigator Hohokam to the south, and mountain dwelling Mogollon to the southeast. No other prehistoric culture in the Southwest had so many different life-styles close at hand from which to pick and choose. And the Sinagua chose freely, creating a distinctive culture in their distinctive environment.

We define their culture by a list of *things:* paddle-smoothed plain brown pottery, timber pit houses (early) and sandstone masonry pueblos (late), cremation and burial with legs extended. But what did they call themselves, and how did they define the differences between their own culture and neighboring Anasazi or Cohonina? Did Sinagua and Hohokam view each other as might a northern Arizonan and a southern Arizonan, a Minnesotan and an Alabaman, or an Eskimo and a Nigerian?

Sinagua lived at the edge of great ponderosa pine forests, in the warmer, more livable climate of the piñon-juniper forest. They planted wherever a layer of cinders

*Dwarfed pine, Bonito Lava Flow,
Sunset Crater*

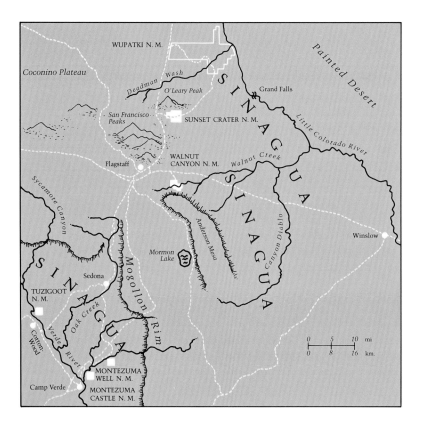

served as mulch, slowing the evaporation of moisture from the soil and allowing Sinagua to dry farm corn, pumpkins, and beans. They traded for their luxuries: Hohokam shell ornaments and Kayenta decorated pottery. Wild plant gathering and hunting still satisfied many of their food needs.

Right up to the time Sunset Crater erupted, Sinagua continued to live in scattered small settlements—concentrating on land around modern Flagstaff where soils were quite moist and in the cinder areas south of present-day Sunset Crater. To be guaranteed sufficient moisture for farming they had to remain at elevations higher than about 6,000 feet, trading the longer growing season of lower elevations for water.

Prior to 1065, few people lived in the area now within Wupatki National Monument, for no cinder mulch existed to allow dry farming in this arid basin and only a few springs provided water. These springs offered home sites for small groups of Kayenta Anasazi, who founded the pueblo which today we call Wupatki.

Then came the end of an era: in 1065 Sunset Crater rained destruction on the northeast Sinagua frontier and Indians living there fled from the black cloud whose sparks ignited the thatched roofs of their homes.

Years passed. The eruption quieted, and the Sinagua began exploring their transformed landscape.

Long familiar with the advantages of cinder-covered farmland, the Sinagua soon discovered the bonanza bestowed by Sunset Crater. Prevailing southwesterly winds had blanketed the land northeast of the crater with ash. Wupatki Basin, previously too dry to make much of a home, now offered the long-sought pairing of cinder-rich soil and a long growing season.

Not only did the cinders retain water in surface soil, but groundwater built up to seep out in springs and along previously dry drainages. At the end of the eleventh century and on into the twelfth, hundreds of small villages sprang up to take advantage of newly created farmland, not only in Wupatki, but also along the southern edge of the ash fall at Walnut Canyon. Movements of Sinagua during this land boom brought new contacts with Hohokam, Anasazi, Mogollon, and Cohonina farmers, and migrant groups of these neighboring cultures may have moved closer to Sinagua territory to share new farmland created by Sunset Crater or to fill gaps left by emigrant Sinagua.

Gradually these cultures blended. Sinagua adopted large villages and Central American-style ball courts from the Hohokam, multistoried masonry pueblos from the Anasazi, and traded other goods and ideas with the newcomers. Intermarriage surely played a vital role. By the mid-1100s, the Sinagua were headed into their climactic years.

As the population of the Wupatki area boomed, crowded Sinagua sought new land and moved into upper Walnut Canyon after 1125. Walnut Canyon National Monument preserves their dwellings—more than 300 small rooms built in the limestone ledges of the canyon. This section of Walnut Canyon offered two attractions: dependable water on the canyon floor and deep recesses along the ledges, where rock overhangs could form the roof and back wall of a room, saving much work for the stonemasons. Fertile land lay within two miles of either rim, close enough to make the canyon a highly desirable home.

In addition, Walnut Canyon provided a wide diversity of plants to use for food, tools, and weapons. Broad-leaved trees like Arizona black walnut, aspen, and willow grew along Walnut Creek. On the cool north-facing slope, ponderosa pine and Douglas fir faced dry south-facing hills cross-canyon, covered with piñon and juniper, yucca and cactus. Such a wide variety of plants offered the Sinagua a ready-made drug and department store at their doorstep.

Lomaki Ruin and the San Francisco Peaks,
Wupatki (left)

Ledge ruins on the Island Trail,
Walnut Canyon (right)

Meanwhile, the Wupatki Sinagua flourished. Wupatki Pueblo grew to three stories, containing more than a hundred rooms with a masonry ball court nearby. The other large pueblos seen today along the Wupatki National Monument road grew to maximum size at this time in the late 1100s.

The golden years were few, however. The gift of the cinders began to lose potency through overintensive farming in the highly populated region. Winds began blowing the evenly-spread ash layers into useless dunes. At first, the Sinagua may simply have concentrated around remaining good land, which would account for the size of the largest pueblos. Then, repeated droughts in the early 1200s led to long water shortages and crop disasters. The Sinagua, forced to leave the Wupatki area only 150 years after they arrived, went looking for water. Wupatki Basin was abandoned by 1250.

A few Sinagua continued to live where they had before the Sunset Crater eruption. Many migrated further, and with their move south to the Verde River valley the Sinagua culture spilled off the south rim of the Colorado Plateau. Along the Verde the Sinagua created a new homeland in the 1200s, building pueblos preserved today at Tuzigoot, Montezuma Castle, and Montezuma Well national monuments. A few of these later Sinagua pueblos existed into the 1400s, when the last urban Sinagua gave up their towns. No current theory reliably documents their whereabouts in historic times.

Today, three national monuments preserve much of the Sinagua story in remarkable detail. Sunset Crater looks little different than it must have looked to the Sinagua. Jagged lava flows stream out from the crater in paths where they coagulated 900 years ago. Heaps of black sand remain bare except for a few rabbitbrush and stunted ponderosa pines.

A paved road leads from Sunset Crater National Monument down through piñon and juniper to the desert scrub and red sandstone and black basalt of Wupatki, where the Painted Desert glows on the horizon. Here the road passes close by several of the largest Sinagua pueblos. This loop is an easy and fascinating alternative to the main route up U.S. 89.

And at Walnut Canyon, a trail leads around an island mesa in the canyon, its ledges full of empty ruins, testimony not only to the passage of time but to the considerable vandalism suffered by the Walnut Canyon ruins in the late 1800s before the national monument was established in 1915.

"The Holy Ghost," Canyonlands

Whatever their original intention, the long-dead artists and hunters confront us across the centuries with the poignant sign of their humanity. I was here, says the artist. We were here, say the hunters.

EDWARD ABBEY, *Desert Solitaire,* 1968

FREMONT

Dinosaur National Monument, Utah/Colorado
Capitol Reef National Park, Utah
Canyonlands National Park, Utah

NORTH OF ANASAZI COUNTRY lived the Fremont Indians, for some 800 years the distinctive culture of the Plateau north of the Colorado River. Named after the Fremont River at Capitol Reef, the Fremont adopted agriculture and pit house architecture before A.D. 500. Their land stretched from the Colorado, Virgin, and Escalante rivers (where they overlapped Anasazi territory) north across all of Utah into adjoining parts of Nevada, Colorado, and possibly Idaho. Fremont people built few masonry pueblos even in their heyday. For this single reason, their presence on the Plateau has inspired much less archaeological research and popular recognition than the Anasazi.

Fremonters lived in the Dinosaur National Monument area until about 950, and these northern people shared many traits with Plains Indians rather than with the Anasazi far to the south. Southern Fremont felt the Anasazi influence strongly after 900, but still maintained their distinctive cultural habits, such as wearing moccasins instead of sandals and relying for their living more on hunting than farming. By 1300, even the southern Fremont had abandoned their homeland. Conflicting theories suggest they migrated to the Great Plains, or simply took up hunting and gathering once more to eventually develop into the historic Paiutes.

Only a few low mounds or rings of foundation stones show where Fremont pit house villages existed, certainly not as romantic a monument to their lives here as the great Anasazi cliff dwellings. Granaries and slab-lined storage pits occur frequently throughout Fremont country. But perhaps most compelling of any remaining trace of Fremont culture is their rock art.

No one knows for certain what meanings lie hidden in prehistoric rock art. Petroglyphs (pecked or carved) and pictographs (painted) occur all over the world; Fremont rock art is as intriguing a collection of inscriptions as can be found anywhere. Dinosaur National Monument and Capitol Reef and Canyonlands national parks preserve some of the best known Fremont petroglyphs and pictographs.

Remarkable representations of manlike beings dominate Fremont rock art. Such figures occur in Anasazi rock art, too, but the Anasazi gave no special emphasis to the human figure. Game animals like bighorn sheep and birds occur in abundance in Anasazi panels, along with many abstract designs. Possible meanings suggested for these Anasazi communications involve hunting rituals, histories of tribal wanderings, and trail markers and guides to water.

Fremont rock art insistently leads you to suspect that you are viewing the religious symbols of a culture dead for 700 years. Only a spiritual meaning can explain the power of these carved and painted beings. Whether the figures represent manlike gods or godlike men—humans decked out in full ceremonial costume—they command attention and respect. Many have painted or tattooed bodies and faces and wear elaborate horned headdresses, as well as kilts, belts, pendants, and necklaces.

Some figures stare mutely from the cliffs. Others hold wild plants, stalk game animals (bison, bighorn, deer), or act out scenes of warfare, complete with huge shields and bows and arrows. In Dinosaur National Monument, beautifully carved figures seem to hold trophy heads, possibly human. Such preoccupation with traditionally male activities suggests that the Fremont men created most of this art.

Among the most mystifying and powerful of Fremont artworks are the somber life-size beings represented at Barrier Canyon (also called Horseshoe Canyon) in Canyonlands National Park, and at other nearby places. These ghostly figures often occur far from major dwelling sites, suggesting that the Fremont may have viewed these locations as special ceremonial centers. Some archaeologists feel these figures predate the Fremont Indians, since their style is quite distinct from other Fremont art. Who painted the Barrier Canyon figures? Perhaps these abstracted gods were the creation of a single inspired artist and his disciples. Or do they form our only remnant from some pre-Fremont culture?

Whether or not we ever discover much about their creators, when in the presence of the Barrier Canyon ghost-men or the headdressed and necklaced Fremont figures, looking out over these canyons we share in the spirit of the long-gone artists. What powers do these painted figures still possess? Perhaps if we knew the proper chant to offer, they could bestow their blessing on us. Maybe our simple respect and protection will stir them to help in keeping the canyons pure, wild, and unpolluted—as good a place for spiritual renewal today as in the times of the Fremont.

Petroglyphs, Island Park, Dinosaur (left)

"The All American Man," Canyonlands (right)

NEYSA DICKEY

PEG JOHNSON

Shearing time for the Navajo flocks

A potter and her artworks, Acoma Pueblo

Navajo woman and hogan

Blue corn harvest, Hopi Pueblos

Interlude: THE PEOPLE

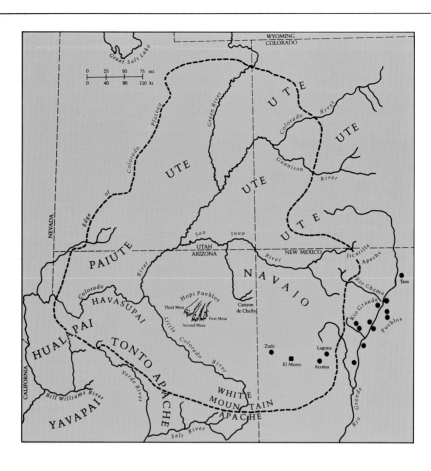

GARY NABHAN

How big do Havasupai sunflowers grow? (left)

Havasu Falls (right)

SHERRY MANGUM

DINEH. PA'A. NUNT'Z. NUWU. These tribal names all mean the same thing: The People. Most American Indian tribes call themselves The People, each seeing themselves as the only *true* people. Rarely do we know tribes by their own names; we call the four tribes above the Navajo, Havasupai and Hualapai (two branches of the Pa'a, or Pai), Ute, and Paiute, respectively.

These four groups reached the Plateau not many centuries before the Spanish and Americans. When freshly arrived, they found themselves newcomers in the ancestral home of the truest Plateau peoples—the Pueblo Indians.

As Anasazi had moved south and east from the Four Corners area after the 1200s, they concentrated in a few pueblos that have continued life in the Anasazi tradition through the twentieth century. Only five pueblo groups remain on the Plateau. Hopi, Zuñi, and Acoma date to at least the twelfth century. The Tewa village of Hano in the Hopi country and Laguna were founded in the late 1600s. Most other Pueblo Indians moved east of the Plateau to the Rio Grande Valley. These five westernmost Plateau pueblos come closest to preserving the Anasazi heritage: to increase the meaning of your visits to Anasazi ruins, travel to Acoma or the Hopi Mesas, too, and meet the descendants of the Anasazi.

Many Hopi men still divide their time between their kivas and their fields, where they dry farm or flashflood-irrigate maize, beans, squash, sunflowers, melons, and grapes. Hopi women still make pottery in the polychrome style of the Kayenta Anasazi —a tradition revived almost singlehandedly in the late 1800s by Nampeyo, a Tewa woman from Hano. Zuñi and Acoma potters not only keep alive the Anasazi pottery styles of corrugation and black-on-white geometric designs, but transcend the old styles as pueblo pottery continues to reflect the artistic growth of its makers.

First to join the pueblos on the Plateau were the Pai, people who long ago moved into the country on the south rim of the Grand Canyon from their ancestral lower Colorado River home. The many Pai bands were split into two groups with the creation of reservations, the Havasupai isolated from the rest of the Hualapai.

Hualapai once lived in tiny settlements at water sources from the Grand Canyon south to the Bill Williams River near modern Parker, Arizona. They irrigated small fields and wandered seasonally to hunt and gather wild food plants. They also functioned as the main traders linking the Hopis and the coast. Their many bands included the Havasu Canyon band, now known as the Havasupai. But Hualapai country lay in the path of advancing "civilization" when Americans pushed the frontier through from California to the mines at Prescott. The Hualapai lost the conflicts of the 1860s, and survived a disastrous one-year internment on the Colorado River.

Today, their reservation includes only the Hualapai Plateau rimming the Grand Canyon, and even with large cattle herds few Hualapai can support themselves from reservation-based resources. Even if they wished to live in the old way, their limited lands simply won't provide food in the desert-wise ways they succeeded with in the past.

The Havasupai live in Havasu Canyon, along the sparkling stream leading into the Grand Canyon from the Coconino Plateau. In fact, the name "Coconino" probably comes from the Hopi name for these people, *Koonina*. Isolated from the destruction wreaked on their Hualapai kin in the 1800s, they came to be regarded as a separate tribe. The Havasupai Reservation has a "Shangri-La" reputation based on its four spectacular waterfalls, but the narrow canyon offers limited fertile farmland and the Havasupai likely will never grow much beyond their present numbers of about three hundred.

Next to move onto the Plateau were nomadic people from the Great Basin who would become the Paiute and Ute nations. These hunter/gatherers arrived shortly after A.D. 1000, and their presence may have been one of the pressures forcing Anasazi and Fremont people to abandon their villages, perhaps not through direct warfare, but through increased competition for scarce resources.

The Paiute Indians gradually came to dominate southwestern Utah, and Arizona north of the Colorado River. They lived much as the Hualapai, farming a little to supplement their hunting and gathering. Though early Spanish and American explorers judged the shy Paiute as primitive, these Indians led a life perfectly adapted to the plant and animal resources available to them. Paiutes survived where the explorers often came close to starvation. Today, Pipe Spring National Monument shares part of the small Kaibab Paiute Reservation.

Northeast of Paiute country, the Utes ranged across all of eastern Utah and western Colorado. The Spanish called these people the "Yuta," a name later commemorated by the state name of Utah. In early times they wandered the mountains in summer in small groups and joined in large bands for the winter. Until the Utes acquired horses in the early 1800s, they resembled their relatives, the Paiutes, in their simple nomadic life. Horses transformed them.

Mounted, they gained the mobility and speed necessary to obtain supplies for permanent large bands. Utes extended their range to the buffalo plains, and became raiders, moving out from the mountains to steal horses, livestock, and slaves from Indians and towns to the south. Today, the southern Utes live on small reservations in southwestern Colorado, the northern Utes along the Green River in the Uinta Basin of Utah—small fragments of their once great domain.

The last great immigration of Indian peoples took place in the early 1500s, when groups of Indians closely related to the people of northern Canada moved south with the buffalo into the plains of New Mexico, then west onto the Plateau. These nomads gradually divided into two primary groups. The Apaches, who lived in the mountains on the eastern and southern edges of the Plateau, largely stuck to their non-agricultural ways, while the more northern groups began to raise a few crops, and came to be called Apaches de Navajo (meaning the Apaches of cultivated fields).

The Apaches remained in the high country, mostly beyond the Plateau. Today, only the Jicarilla Apache Reservation lies on the Plateau, in New Mexico, where the Jicarillas were moved from their ancestral home near Taos.

The Navajo slowly grew apart from other Apaches. When Pueblo Indians took refuge near bands of Navajo after their 1680 rebellion against the Spanish, the Navajo absorbed many Pueblo cultural traits: weaving, sheepherding, ceremonial and religious beliefs. Sheepherding became the most distinctive element of the Navajo lifestyle. The Navajo gradually moved westward into what we now think of as Navajo Country, reaching Canyon de Chelly in the 1700s. Then in the 1800s, they began to rely on raids for their supply of sheep and horses.

Not only did they raid New Mexican villages, but former Pueblo allies as well. Navajo raids on the Hopis made permanent enemies of the two tribes. When the United States gained control of the Southwest in the 1840s, it faced a real challenge in making peace with the Navajos. Not until 1864, when Kit Carson (the old mountain man then a U.S. Army colonel) destroyed Navajo sheep, fields, and orchards in Canyon de Chelly, killing no one but destroying their means of livelihood, did the Navajo surrender.

The United States sent eight thousand of the ten thousand or so Navajos on the "Long Walk" to Fort Sumner, southeast of Santa Fe, and tried to make farmers of them. The attempt failed, and after four years the Navajos returned home, gradually rebuilding their lives and their flocks. The imprisonment had forged them into a cultural entity like no previous experience—the only time in tribal history that so many Navajos lived so close together. The old independence surged to life again after their return, but the success of the Navajo today as an organized, unified tribe owes much to shared memories of their four years of captivity, and continuing constant pressures from the non-Indian world.

National parks on the Plateau all lie in the traditional range of one or more of these groups of Native Americans. Most conspicuous in their ties to the parks are the Navajos, who still live in Canyon de Chelly, who still trade at Hubbell Trading Post, whose reservation includes Rainbow Bridge and Navajo national monuments, and whose culture permeates the land from the Grand Canyon to Mesa Verde, from Glen Canyon to Petrified Forest.

The legends and religions of native Plateau peoples speak of many park landmarks. The Hopi believe they emerged into this world through the "Sipapu" in the Grand Canyon; Sunset Crater is the home of their Kana-a Kachina. To the Navajos, Petrified Forest's stone logs are the bones of Yietso, the terrible Giant killed by Monster-Slayer. Rainbow Bridge is a married pair of petrified Rainbow-People, gods helpful in bringing rain to the Navajo.

Some native names have been retained for parks—the Hopi Wupatki, the Ute Hovenweep, the Spanish corruption of the Navajo *tsegi* (rock canyon) at Canyon de Chelly. But Indian words don't roll easily off Anglo tongues, and most have been replaced by lackluster substitutes. Paiutes called Bryce Canyon *Unka-timpe-wa-wince-pock-ich,* meaning "Red rocks standing like men in a bowl-shaped canyon." Zion Canyon was the Paiute's *Ioogoon:* "arrow quiver," or "Come out the way you came in."

Whatever names we use, we owe much of our knowledge of the Plateau to the Native Americans who lived here before our arrival. They discovered the landmarks, first explained their origins, and guided Spanish and Anglo explorers to the sacred places. When we speak of Plateau people, we must acknowledge the Indians as the people closest to the land, truly The People in each of their homelands.

Farm machinery, Candy Ranch, Capitol Reef

Part Three: THE CONQUEST

The tiny oases huddle in their pockets in the rock, surrounded on all sides by as terrible and beautiful wasteland as the world can show, colored every color of the spectrum . . . Man is an interloper in that country, not merely because he maintains a toehold only on sufferance, depending on the precarious and sometimes disastrous flow of desert rivers, but because everything he sees is a prophecy of his inconsequent destiny.

WALLACE STEGNER, *Mormon Country*, 1942

The fort, Pipe Spring

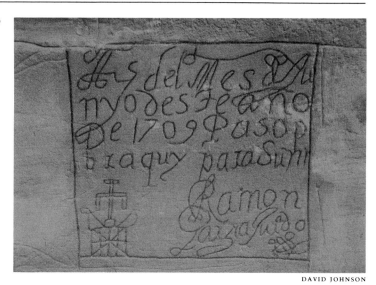

People have been looking into this country for a long time, loving it, cursing it, gutting it, changing it, enduring it. Not all have found it to be beautiful. Many have come to know parts of it very well; few have come to know all of it.

C. GREGORY CRAMPTON, *Standing Up Country, 1964*

DAVID JOHNSON

PIONEERS

El Morro National Monument, New Mexico
Pipe Spring National Monument, Arizona
Hubbell Trading Post National Historic Site, Arizona

PLATEAU HISTORY BEGINS with a swaggering Moorish slave named Estevan and a mythical kingdom named Cibola. Estevan turned up in northern Mexico in 1536 after eight years of wandering through the Southwest with his companion Cabeza de Vaca. They had been shipwrecked on the Gulf of Mexico and brought home with them tales that fired Spanish passions: seven golden cities far to the north, ripe for plundering.

In 1539, Estevan led the Franciscan Fray Marcos de Niza north to Cibola, which turned out to be the six villages at Zuñi Pueblo. The Zuñis killed Estevan, and Fray Marcos returned to Mexico, somehow convinced that indeed he had discovered Cibola.

The next year Francisco Vásquez de Coronado returned to conquer Cibola, and in taking the simple adobe and stone pueblo of Zuñi he discovered that the golden cities might have been an invention of Estevan's fertile imagination. He kept his hopes up while completing the first great exploration of the Southwest, including a look at the Grand Canyon and visits to Hopi and Acoma pueblos.

The Spanish continued to penetrate northward, and in 1598, Juan de Oñate founded the first Spanish settlement in New Mexico. Oñate made long trips through Pueblo country, and passed a great bluff with a large natural pool of rainwater and melted snow each time he traveled the Zuñi-Acoma trail. In 1605, on his return from his discovery of the Gulf of California, he carved news of his trip in the bluff's soft sandstone. Oñate scrawled his message here two years before the founding of Jamestown, fifteen years before the Pilgrims landed at Plymouth Rock.

His inscription marked the first use by the Spanish of a rock register started centuries before by the Pueblo Indians and continued centuries afterward by the Spanish, Mexicans, and Americans. El Morro National Monument preserves this record—the entire span of Plateau history carved in the rock of El Morro (Spanish for "the bluff") by the very people who lived that history.

Early Spanish inscriptions tell of trips to found missions at Hopi and Zuñi—and then trips to avenge the deaths of priests killed by the independent Pueblo people. In 1680 the Pueblos expelled the Spanish, but in 1692 De Vargas reconquered them—leaving his proud inscription at El Morro: "Here was the General Don Diego de Vargas who conquered for our Holy Faith, and for the Royal Crown, all of New Mexico at his own expense, year of 1692."

The last Spanish inscription at El Morro dates to 1774. The 1800s brought American explorers who added their names to Inscription Rock, along with assorted pioneers, soldiers, traders, and Indian agents. Today, the historic graffiti on the bluff at El Morro can be reached easily by following a paved road into the Zuñi Mountains from Interstate 40 at Gallup or Grants.

In 1774, when the Spanish record ends at El Morro, the missionary priest at Zuñi was one Fray Silvestre Vélez de Escalante. Two years later Fray Escalante would pass El Morro on the last leg of a major journey of exploration, the first Spanish penetration of the Plateau heartland—the Canyon Country. With Fray Francisco Atanasio Domínguez and ten other men, Escalante set out from Santa Fe in 1776 to attempt to find a direct overland route to California. They traveled in a great circle, north through western Colorado, then turning west and crossing the Green River just below Split Mountain in Dinosaur National Monument. At Utah Lake, near modern Provo, they turned south and skirted the west edge of the Plateau past Zion. They aptly named the Virgin River the *Rio Sulfureo de las Piramides*, the last word surely commemorating the stone "pyramids" of Zion.

Finally, they gave up on California and turned back toward New Mexico. They found their way across the Colorado River at a point not far above today's Glen Canyon Dam, a ford forever after known as the Crossing of the Fathers (today flooded by Lake Powell). Then to Hopi to Zuñi to Acoma and on to Santa Fe.

No new Spanish missions came of the Domínguez-Escalante expedition. Spain already had extended its frontiers to their maximum and soon would begin to pull back. In the early 1800s, New Mexican traders and American fur trappers explored the Plateau, spending more time in the Uinta Basin and High Plateaus than in the more rugged Canyon Country or Grand Canyon area. The earliest records we have from the deeper canyons are three 1836 inscriptions left by the mysterious Denis Julien in Labyrinth, Stillwater, and Cataract canyons. Probably a mountain man in search of beaver, we know nothing more of Julien, though he may have been the first through these canyons by boat.

The 1840s and 1850s saw the Plateau begin to come into focus in the minds of Americans—and on their maps. Topographic engineers and railroad surveyors described Chaco Canyon, Canyon de Chelly, Petrified Forest, and Wupatki. Army expeditions reached The Needles in Canyonlands and the bottom of the Grand Canyon at Diamond Creek. John Wesley Powell's river expeditions in 1869 and 1872, and subsequent overland explorations by Powell and his co-workers A. H. Thompson, G. K. Gilbert, and Clarence Dutton, climaxed the official surveys of the Plateau.

In 1847, the Mormons arrived in Utah and soon began to colonize south into the Plateau from Salt Lake City. At Moab, Utes beat back the first Mormon settlement in 1855. Paiutes allowed successful Mormon colonies along the base of the High Plateaus near Zion about the same time. In 1858, Brigham Young sent the great Mormon trailblazer Jacob Hamblin on the first Mormon mission to the Hopis. On this and subsequent trips, Hamblin opened the road from St. George, Utah, south into Arizona.

On his first trip, Hamblin camped at a spring at the base of the Vermilion Cliffs just south of the present Utah-Arizona line. Legend says that here his brother, "Gunlock" Will Hamblin, when teased into proving his reputation for fine marksmanship, shot the bottom out of a pipe bowl at fifty paces without touching the sides. True or not, the spring became Pipe Spring from then on.

By 1863, a Mormon rancher by the name of James Whitmore had taken up residence at Pipe Spring and soon he ran respectable herds of cattle and sheep. Unfortunately for Whitmore, he arrived on the Mormon frontier at the same time that the Navajo frontier reached this same area.

Those Navajo who had escaped the "Long Walk" and internment at Fort Sumner in 1864 had fled to Monument Valley and west past Navajo Mountain to the Colorado River—wild country safe from pursuit, and new territory for the Navajos. They needed food, and the Mormon herds were close and tempting.

In the next several years Navajo raids across the Colorado for sheep and cattle reached the proportions of war. Early 1866 ended James Whitmore's stay at Pipe Spring: Navajos killed him and made off with his sheep. Later that year the Mormons abandoned all settlements east of Pipe Spring, and in 1868 the Mormon militia made the spring their headquarters, building a rock house near Whitmore's dugout.

But in 1869, Navajo raids stopped. The Fort Sumner Reservation had failed and the surviving Navajos were returning home with promises of food and livestock to get the tribe back on their feet. In 1870, Brigham Young himself journeyed to Pipe Spring to look over prospects for resettlement. On his arrival he happened on John Wesley Powell and Jacob Hamblin, the latter guiding Powell in his search for the three men who had left his 1869 river expedition in lower Grand Canyon. This meeting in the wilderness of three men who left strong personal imprints on Plateau history must have been memorable.

Pipe Spring soon became a successful Mormon outpost. A rock fort enclosed the spring—nicknamed Winsor Castle after Anson Winsor, the first man in charge of the great cattle herds. Through the 1870s and 1880s the Pipe Spring herd produced beef and, especially, milk which the residents of the fort made into butter and cheese to be shipped to St. George. The great cooperative herds badly overgrazed the fragile desert grassland, however, and the Pipe Spring herd passed to individual ranchers before establishment of the fort as a national monument in 1923. Today, a summer visit to the monument brings to life the 1880s frontier, as the Park Service re-creates life at Pipe Spring, right down to the cheese-making.

The Mormons moved swiftly to settle the rest of the inhabitable Canyon Country once Navajo raids ended. By 1880, they were farming bottomlands along the Paria below Bryce, on the Fremont in Capitol Reef, on the headwaters of the Escalante, and along the Price River below the Book Cliffs. In 1880 they blasted their way across the Colorado River in Glen Canyon, creating the famous Hole-in-the-Rock, and pushed through to the San Juan River to found Bluff.

Approaching the Mormon-Navajo frontier from the other side, in 1870 Juan Lorenzo Hubbell left his home in New Mexico at the age of seventeen to seek his future in the new territory to the west. After several years of working for Indian traders in Utah and Arizona and serving as Spanish interpreter for the Navajos in their last peace negotiations with Jacob Hamblin, Hubbell set up his own trading business. He chose a valley deep in Navajo country, not far east of the Hopi villages. Lorenzo named the spot Ganado, after his friend the Navajo chief Ganado Mucho. By 1879, he had bought a permanent trading post, filed a homestead claim (since this was not yet reservation land), and gotten married.

Along with other traders to the Navajo, Hubbell provided many services. He traded supplies—coffee, flour, sugar, candy, Pendleton blankets, tobacco, calico, pocket-knives, and canned goods—for Navajo wool and lambs, silverwork, and hand-woven blankets and rugs. He served as advisor, translator, emergency doctor, peacemaker, teacher, and friend to the Indians who traded at Ganado, the most important contact with the non-Indian world for most of them.

Cattle drive, Capitol Reef

Doorway plaque, Hubbell Trading Post

Juan Lorenzo Hubbell, 1906 *(courtesy of The Southwest Museum)*

Hubbell and his sons gradually built a trading empire that included at various times whole or part ownership of twenty-four trading posts, as well as stage lines, freight lines, and a warehouse in Winslow. Hubbell served as Apache County sheriff in the midst of a range war, legislator during Arizona's transition from territory to state, and host to what seemed like every traveler in northern Arizona. Among his favorites in those he entertained at Ganado were Theodore Roosevelt, and the artist E. A. Burbank, whose best work crowds the walls of the Hubbell home.

Whites called Hubbell "Don Lorenzo," and knew him for his complete honesty in business. The Navajos called him "Double Glasses" for his thick spectacles, and "Old Mexican," with respect. Hubbell did much to stimulate quality in Navajo weaving and silver. His fondness for large blankets—nine by twelve feet or even larger—encouraged the transition in Navajo textiles from blanket to rug. "Ganado Red" still refers to rugs woven along Hubbell's tastes: large, well-made, a predominance of cross and diamond designs, and usually a background of red.

Hubbell's grand hospitality toned down somewhat in later years, with the death of his wife, an expensive unsuccessful run for the United States Senate, and business reverses. Don Lorenzo died in 1930, after trading at Ganado for fifty years. He first came to the Navajos only two years after their return from the "Long Walk," and served as their faithful friend through their many years of adjustment to the crossfire pressures of reservation life and gradually encroaching white culture. When he died, the importance of the old-time Indian trader was decreasing; auto transportation had begun to make a dent in the isolation of the reservation interior.

Within twenty years after Hubbell's death the Navajos entered a new era. Uranium and oil booms after World War II brought money to replace horse-drawn wagons with pickup trucks. Flagstaff and Gallup became easy shopping trips.

The Hubbell family realized that the Ganado trading post had become a historic remnant of a time all but disappeared. In 1967, the trading post became a national historic site, to insure preservation of at least one traditional trading post. Today, the post still functions as an important element in the community, particularly in trading for crafts: Hubbell's offers for sale fine Navajo rugs and silver, and the work of Pueblo artists, as well.

The Park Service provides tours of the Hubbell home, a wonderfully comfortable building that conveys the force and character of Don Lorenzo's personality: huge Navajo rugs cover every floor, bed, and piece of furniture; baskets from all over the Southwest fill the ceiling between great beams; heavy-framed paintings mosaic every wall; and books overflow their shelves. Here Don Lorenzo Hubbell lived a life that bridged the swift evolution from Navajo raiders and American explorers to the very brink of the present.

Today, we have passed that brink and find ourselves on the new brink of an uncertain future. Where will Plateau history lead next?

Four Corners Power Plant

MICHAEL COLLIER

Finale: THE PROSPECT

TO SAVE A WILDLAND, CONSERVATIONISTS have to win their political battle over and over and over again. They can't lose once, for a loss is final. As wilderness becomes rare in the world, and therefore more precious, the Colorado Plateau wilderness has become a major battleground between conservationists and developers.

Besides scenery and wild country and clean air, the Plateau contains coal, uranium, oil, natural gas, and oil shale. But the minerals aren't easily freed from this rock desert. Transportation difficulties make mining here exhausting and expensive. That's why the Plateau wilderness has survived as long as it has. Here the early mining booms never reached the stage of intense technology which led to serious damage to the land.

Although more famous gold rushes happened in the West, the Canyon Country, too, saw thorough exploration by prospectors in the late 1800s. First they searched for legendary silver mines, famous since the days of the Spanish. Then in 1883, a placer gold strike in Glen Canyon brought hundreds of miners into the Colorado and San Juan canyons, trying hard to make the superfine gold dust pay off. Robert Brewster Stanton—once proponent and surveyor of a riverbank railroad along the Colorado River from the Rockies to the ocean—installed a huge gold dredge that didn't work. By 1911 the rugged Canyon Country had discouraged the most dream-filled prospectors and the gold rush ended.

Oil, copper, and radium kept miners busy for several more decades. While miners explored side canyons from the rivers, cattlemen worked down canyons from the rangelands above. Gradually the canyons divulged their secrets: natural bridges, ruins, arches. The most spectacular treasures became widely known and then protected in national parks and monuments.

Three resources have shaped recent Plateau history more than any others: water, coal, and uranium. The uranium boom following World War II created the greatest mining rush to the Plateau. After a period of relative calm, today the uranium hunt is on again.

Problems associated with water and coal development, however, put the Plateau's wild places in greatest peril. The rivers of the Plateau make tempting sources for hydroelectric power, and their naturally erratic seasonal flows make them prime candidates for control by engineers seeking to "store" water to even out its downstream availability through the year. Hoover Dam came first, completed in 1935 and for the first time pooling the water of the mighty Colorado.

In the 1950s attempts to dam the Green in Dinosaur National Monument were thwarted; the Green was tamed upstream, at Flaming Gorge. But in 1956 conservationists lost the battle to save Glen Canyon and in 1963, the dam was completed and Lake Powell began to fill. The 1960s also saw completion of dams on the upper San Juan and Gunnison rivers.

Most of these dams serve important, useful functions. But Plateau dams have a relatively short life expectancy: they silt up fast. We must weigh their period of usefulness against the special worth of the land they permanently destroy. Two dams proposed for the Grand Canyon, for instance, have been avoided several times—and probably will be proposed again and (hopefully) delayed again. It seems the engineers hold no place sacred, not even the Grand Canyon.

And then there is coal. The Plateau holds vast reserves of this black energy-rich mineral, and has yielded millions of tons from the High Plateaus and Book Cliffs near Price, Utah, and more recently, from the Navajo Country. Nine huge coal-fired power plants now encircle the Plateau parks, with many more plants in planning stages. Pollutants from these plants merge as they drift across the once-crystalline air of the parklands, frequently casting a brown pall across views in Grand Canyon, Canyonlands, Bryce Canyon, Mesa Verde, and other areas.

On a map of the Plateau find what appears to be the central point, the focus of concentration of parks, the heart of the land we value enough to protect. Your finger likely will come to rest near Glen Canyon—which we've already destroyed. Quite possibly your central spot will fall along a narrow, wild plateau just north of Glen Canyon—a plateau with the magical name of Kaiparowits.

The Kaiparowits Plateau harbors billions of tons of coal. It also is a wild, beautiful place, in itself deserving of protection but also a wilderness buffer for the national parks surrounding it. The giant energy corporations hold leases on Kaiparowits coal, and naturally wish to mine it and profit from their leases. So they propose scheme after scheme in hopes of getting a start on Kaiparowits mining—eager for any beachhead that allows them to begin development. At one time their proposal involved strip mining and a mine-mouth power plant that would have been the world's largest.

These days they want to deep-mine the coal and ship it out by railway—or truck it out through Bryce Canyon National Park if they can't build the new railroad. The market for the coal: California (which may not even need it), and Japan.

Industrialization of Plateau parks country on this gigantic scale would create high-crime boom towns, destroy rural life-styles, accelerate overcrowding of park resources, endanger fragile back-country with hordes of off-road vehicles, pollute the air, obliterate the silence, and erase the wild spirit of the land. Pot-hunting and vandalism to rock art, already a severe problem on the Plateau, would deplete archaeological resources at an even more rapid rate. Wildlife requiring remote, undisturbed habitats to reproduce successfully (desert bighorn and peregrine falcons, to name two) would disappear.

Kaiparowits isn't the only place where planned developments endanger survival of park values. Strip mines have been proposed on the borders of Bryce Canyon and Capitol Reef national parks; plans for power plants are well along for locations just upwind from Zion and at the head of the Escalante River basin, one of the largest intact remnants of slickrock wilderness on the Plateau.

How badly do we need Colorado Plateau coal?

How much of our wilderness heritage will we sacrifice forever to obtain energy for the next few years?

Where will we go to renew our spirits when we have transformed the Colorado Plateau from a shining, wild, bright edge of the world to an industrialized, polluted, crowded, and dying land?

Where will we draw the line?

Navajo woman at sunrise

JOHN RUNNING